Feb

MW00679614

Laura

Love,

Norma

Journal
of the
Little Girls

a memoir
of childhood sexual abuse
and healing

Norma Jean Willmott

ISBN 978-0-615-77517-3

Dedicated to my husband, Dan, for always being there for me, and for holding me as I cried so hard, and to my children Jared, Stephanie, Scott, Stacy and Wendy for helping me in the only way they could—by showing me unconditional love.

CONTENTS

INTRODUCTION

My journal was written to aid me in my healing. As I put on paper my thoughts and my feelings, it helps to release them and to set me free.

I have been honest as I have shared with the reader all of my emotions and memories. If this book is difficult to understand in some places, it is because I have been dealing with what seemed like two different people, the adult Norma and the Little Girl, as they have been striving to become one. My memories and emotions have not come back in chronological order. Sometimes memories would come back before the emotions. More often the emotions came before the memories. I could be recovering from one emotion and have a memory of something else the same day. Most of my memories have been of a three- or four-year-old child. Later in my healing I learned of the Older Girls who were also a part of my memories and emotions.

As I was recovering, I searched the bookstores for accounts of other people who endured what I was going through. The more I read of other survivors and their victories, the more encouraged I became.

It is my hope that anyone who reads this book and is suffering from repressed memories and emotions will be aided in their recovery.

PROLOGUE

I have heard, "Repressed memories are just another false syndrome. Repressed memories are only an excuse for the things you are doing wrong today. Repressed memories are only a way for therapists to make money."

While I was healing, my older sister, Bonnie, said to me that the things I was remembering could not have occurred in our home without anyone knowing that it was happening. My memories, she believed, must have come from the books that I read and the programs I had watched on television. She believed it was a false syndrome.

Hearing this attack of repressed memories from the media and from family members hinders a person who is indeed suffering from repressed memories. Repressed memories do exist.

As survivors, we must do our best to help ourselves. As we read how others have survived this very difficult journey, it encourages us and helps us to know that we can also succeed. It does not give us memories. It helps us to understand the memories we are now experiencing.

At the time my memories began I was a 49-year-old woman. I had nothing to make excuses for in my past. I had been married at the age of 23. By the time I was 35 years old I had five happy children. I was active in my church and community. I have held positions of responsibility and teaching.

When I was 36 years old I began to do strange things. When I was frustrated, I would go into my bedroom, shut the door and cry very hard while slapping my face. I would hit myself over and over again until my face was red with handprints on it. Once I calmed down, the rest of the day would be as any other regular day in my life. As I thought of these actions later, after recovering my memories, I realized that when my strange behavior began my three daughters were the same age as my two sisters and I were when the abuse began in my life.

When I was 40 years old I became very depressed. For almost a year I stayed in my house as much as possible. I could go to work without any problems, but as soon as I returned home I seemed to go into a shell. I could not drive my daughters to their Brownie meeting because I was afraid a parent would come out to my car to talk to me. This fear became so strong that if Dan didn't get home from work in time to take the girls, I would literally become ill. I would panic, and be sick to my stomach. If I were alone at church I would sit in the back row so I could hurry out, in case someone would come to talk to me. If my family was with me I was not quite so frightened. My son, Scott, in later years said to me, "Mom, you left the Pack Meeting before I received my Arrow of Light Award." That hurt him deeply and I was not even aware of it at the time. All I knew was that I had to get out of that room. Dan was the Scoutmaster and was participating in the program, leaving me to sit alone.

I believe it is important to note here that I have never been on medication for my memories and that my memories began before I saw a therapist. I have never been hypnotized, and I have never had a memory in a therapist's office. I have always been alone or with a family member when a memory returned. The role of my therapist was to aid me in dealing with my daily life as I was recovering.

When I was 47 years old my life changed. The following pages tell the story.

CHAPER 1

PENNY

October 11, 1992

This morning I received a phone call from my sister, Penny. "Can you come over right away?" She was crying and was very upset as she talked to me.

"Of course I can! I will be there in a few minutes," I replied to her. "Let me come with you," Dan said to me.

When we arrived at Penny's home, Robin, her daughter, said, "mom and dad are upstairs in their bedroom. You can go right up."

As we climbed the stairs, I wondered what might be wrong. We found Penny sitting on a chair next to her bed with Bob standing beside her.

Bob said, "Penny has something she wants to talk to you about, Norma." Then Penny tearfully spoke, "I think I was sexually abused as a child."

When she said this, thoughts began racing through my mind. Penny had had emotional problems for many years. She could never stand to be alone. She could not even drive her car by herself. When we were children, our home was across the street from the elementary school that Penny attended, and her classroom faced our house. She could see from her classroom when my mother drove the car out of our driveway, and she would become hysterical. She had to be transferred to another classroom where she could not see our house.

Penny continued to cry as she talked to me. "I think it was Daddy. Every time I kiss Bob I see daddy's face. I hate to have Bob touch me. One night I was lying on the floor and Bob came up to me and touched my breast. I jumped and screamed, "No daddy, don't do that."

She told me that she remembered daddy kissing her and putting his tongue in her mouth. "It was so awful," she said.

I believed her immediately. I was not surprised at what she told me. All the time Penny was talking to us I remained very calm.

As soon as I returned home, I fell apart. I went into my bathroom and sat at the edge of my tub. I started to cry softly, but I could not stop crying. My gentle tears became a flood as they came harder and harder until exhaustion stopped them.

My life changed after my conversation with Penny. Any little thing would set me off on a crying spell. Not just a little cry, but uncontrollable sobbing.

I said to Dan on different occasions, "I don't think it happened to me."

October 20, 1992

I was at Penny's house today. She was very emotional. She said she wanted to tell mom about the abuse. She was nervous about confronting her. She felt more comfortable having mom come to her home than for her to go to our parents' house. I went to mom's house and told her she needed to come with me for a ride. I said that dad needed to stay home. All the way to Penny's house she kept asking me what was wrong. She figured out we were going to Penny's. I just told her she had to wait.

When we arrived at Penny's home, she was sitting in the dining room crying. Mom was very upset by now. Penny said to mom, "I was sexually abused as a child. The person who abused me was daddy."

My mother seemed shocked and immediately said that it must have been someone else. "Maybe you are not remembering correctly." Penny told her she remembered clearly the things he had done to her.

Mom's reply was, "Maybe he did some things he shouldn't have, but he didn't do it all." Her next comment was, "What would people think if they knew!"

November 4, 1992

Today I had trouble with my car. I was in the garage and the car wouldn't start. For some reason I felt helpless. I felt frustrated. I went into my bedroom and sat on my bed. I started to cry. Soon I was sobbing. I realized after a while that I was not crying like a normal adult. I was sitting on my bed, shoulders bent down, with my head almost to my stomach. My actions went from my fingers being in my mouth to wringing my hands like a little child. I continued to cry very hard. After a little while I thought to myself, "Norma, what is going on here? You are acting like a very young child. You are 47 years old, acting like a three-year-old." This upset me very much. I could not understand my gestures and feelings of helplessness. All from car trouble in the garage.

November 15, 1992

My husband, children and I have always gone to church together on Sundays. Today I was so emotionally distressed that I couldn't go. I could not stand the thought of having to speak to anyone. I was home alone and became very despondent. I sat in my bedroom. I knew that we had a bottle of Motrin in the medicine cabinet. I started thinking about taking all of them. I went to the medicine cabinet and looked at the bottle. Then I took the bottle and held it in my hand for almost an hour, wondering if I should take them. When I realized it was almost time for my family to return home I put them back into the medicine cabinet.

I don't understand why I am so depressed. All of these strange actions of mine began with my talk with Penny. Does it have anything to do with her memories?

CHAPTER 2

REACH FOR THE RAINBOW

November 18, 1992

I went to a bookstore today and was browsing. I seemed to know that there was a book I needed to read, but I had no idea what I was looking for. I came to a shelf of self-help books, and I saw *Reach for the Rainbow*. The cover read: *Advanced Healing for Survivors of Sexual Abuse*. I purchased it and took it home with me. I felt it might help me in dealing with Penny's memories. The author, Lynne D. Finney, is a woman who had been abused as a child and had repressed her memories for many years.

Even though I was reading this book to help me aid Penny, while I was reading I could see myself in it. I could not put the book down. I felt a kinship with the author. This book helped me keep my sanity as I went through the process of remembering my abusive years.

November 22, 1992

My daily life has become one of tears. I cry over everything. I not only cry, I CRY!! I cannot understand my actions. Penny knows my father abused her. I believe her. I cannot understand why this is so difficult for me. In some ways it seems to be affecting me more than her.

Whenever I cry Dan holds me in his arms and comforts me. He has become insistent that we talk with my father. He thinks it may help to clear up the mystery and enable Penny and me to recover sooner.

November 24, 1992

I have had a more difficult time sleeping at night than usual. I have always had to read or watch television until I fall asleep, but it is much worse now. I sometimes wake up in the middle of the night and will be awake for two or three hours before going back to sleep. In the morning, after all the children are at school and Dan is at work, I go back to bed and finally sleep soundly and peacefully.

As I have been reading *Reach for the Rainbow,* I have been thinking about my childhood. I try to remember childhood memories. I don't remember much of my childhood. I have never thought about it before. Dan speaks of his childhood. I'm surprised that he remembers so much. I remember school. I remember my teachers. I just don't remember home.

CHAPTER 3

THANKSGIVING REUNION

November 25, 1992

Penny and I decided to visit our older sister Bonnie in Marietta, Georgia, for Thanksgiving this year. It will be our first time together since Penny shared her memories with me. Bob and Dan have to stay at home because of work obligations. My five teenage children are coming with Penny and me.

November 27, 1992

It is the day after Thanksgiving. Bonnie, George, her husband, and Penny and I went out to lunch. It is the first time we have been together without our children since we arrived in Georgia. We can now talk about Penny's memories.

Once lunch was over, we sat in the restaurant talking. It was about 3:00 in the afternoon. The restaurant was nearly empty. Someone mentioned in the course of our conversation our mother, wondering why she didn't know what had been going on.

I felt a change come over my eyes. I really don't know how to express this fully, except that I literally felt a change in my eyes. I said, "She knew, she knew! I told her. She knew!" Then I began to cry. I completely broke down and sobbed right there in the restaurant. I felt like someone else had been speaking through my mouth. I knew what was being said, but I didn't know where it was coming from. The waiter noticed my distress and came over to our table with a glass of water for me. The bill was quickly paid and we left.

As soon as we got into Bonnie and George's van I began to cry again. Bonnie and George are both wheelchair users and have a specially-equipped van. Penny was sitting in the back seat with me, and Bonnie and George both turned their chairs around to face us. I started to rock, from my waist up, back and forth, sobbing all the while. I rocked and rocked, and then I began to speak, still rocking. I was speaking as a little girl would speak, not as the adult that I am.

I'm not jealous of you Penny. You have to believe that I am not jealous. I'm not jealous of you! I'm really not jealous of you."

By the end of this part of the conversation I was very agitated, and I had to be sure that Penny understood what I was saying.

Penny replied, "Of course you are not jealous of me, Norma. It's okay."

I looked Penny in the eyes as we were talking. It was very important for me to know that she believed me—believed that I was not jealous of her.

I love you. I'm not jealous of you because you are the pretty one and I'm the ugly one, but I'm not jealous. You have to believe me that I am not jealous. Penny, I love you. I'm not jealous of you! I'm so ugly! I'm so ugly!"

After this scene I covered my face with my hands and cried. I continued:

I'm ugly! I'm ugly, I'm ugly.

Penny took her hands and gently removed my hands from my face. She looked me straight in the eyes and said very seriously, "You are not ugly, Norma."

I'm ugly! But I have pretty blue eyes.

I'm ugly was said in a determined angry voice. When I said that I have pretty blue eyes, I was a Little Girl pleased with something nice about herself. I remembered being told by someone that I had pretty blue eyes.

I love Aunt Norma. You have Aunt Norma's eyes. I see Aunt Norma when I see you.

I was seeing Penny with my child's eyes and she looked like Aunt Norma to me. The adult Norma was with me here also because I was confused about how Penny could look like Aunt Norma when I knew that she was my aunt through marriage.

I wanted Aunt Norma to be my mother. Why couldn't Aunt Norma be my mother? Oh why couldn't Aunt Norma be my mother? I was named after her you know.

This was said in a sweet Little Girl's voice.

Then they told me I wasn't named after her! I wanted to be named after her!

Here I became very angry because I was not named after my Aunt Norma.

*I love Aunt Norma. Why couldn't she be my mother? I
wouldn't get you in trouble Penny. I love you. Everyone
knew I was the ugly one.*

This conversation was very difficult for me to understand. I was saying things, yet I had no idea where they were coming from. They came out of my mouth and out of my mind, but I had no idea that they were there in the first place. I felt and expressed anger and frustration. Sometimes I would talk like a Little Girl telling a secret. Sometimes there would be love in my voice. I felt a sad love for Penny, like I had failed her, and a warm love for Aunt Norma.

When I finally stopped rocking and began speaking like an adult, the first thing I said was, "I need a Pepsi!"

Bonnie laughed and said, "How about a Coke. We're just outside of Atlanta, and it is almost impossible to buy a Pepsi anywhere." I settled for a Coke.

I was completely exhausted and confused after my ordeal. We went back to Bonnie's home where Penny cut and colored my hair. We talked for a while, and then we all went to bed early. It had been a difficult day for each of us.

CHAPTER 4

WHO IS THE LITTLE GIRL?

November 29, 1992

We arrived home this afternoon from our reunion with Bonnie. The Little Girl has made herself known again. I was resting in the bathtub. The warm water had a soothing effect on me.

I began to cry, and Dan came into the bathroom to see what the matter was. My crying worked into sobbing. I was sitting in the bathtub rocking back and forth and crying very loudly. This was quite a shock for Dan. I cry easily, often, to release my tensions: soft, gentle tears. Not the emotional trauma I was displaying here. My hands were covering my face as Dan was trying to comfort me, when I said,

I'm dirty and ugly. I don't want to be dirty. I'm really not jealous of Penny. You have to believe that. I love Penny. She's my sister. My mama is not happy. No matter what I do I cannot make my mama happy! It is my fault that she is not happy. When he is with me he is not with Penny.

My emotions would fluctuate rapidly from anger to shame to sadness to frustration and back to shame. Dan told me that I alternated from being the Little Girl to talking to the Little Girl.

"You are not dirty or ugly, Norma," Dan spoke tenderly to me.

I replied, "You have to tell the Little Girl! You have to tell the Little Girl!"

At this time I was very distressed that he was talking to me and not to the Little Girl.

Dan addressed the Little Girl. "Little Girl, you are a good Little Girl. You are a pretty Little Girl. You have to go to sleep now." Dan was worried that I might revert permanently to this Little Girl.

"Let me talk to her, Dan," I said.

I recognized that the Little Girl was me! I saw her with my mind's eye. I saw a little blond girl with blue eyes. "You are not an ugly little girl. You are a pretty little girl." I was so surprised that she was me and that she was not ugly.

I told Dan that the Little Girl was sad and that she just wanted to be happy. I said to the Little Girl, "You have to go to sleep now, Little Girl. I will take care of you. I will not let anything ever happen to you again. Someday you will be happy." I felt as though I was tucking a small child into her bed and tiptoeing out of the room. Only this was all going on in my mind instead of physically happening.

I don't understand how I can know what the Little Girl is feeling. How do I know that she is sad and just wants to be happy? I don't feel like these conversations with the Little Girl are memories. They seem to be emotions coming from somewhere, somewhere inside of me. Everything that is happening to me is so confusing. I don't understand most of what I am thinking.

CHAPTER 5

SHARED MEMORIES

December 1992

Penny spoke of my father kissing her. She was about nine years old and I was eleven. I remember it this way.

We were living in the small town of Elsa, Texas. We lived in a large white house. There was a sidewalk from our house to the garage. There were palm trees in our yard and beautiful red flowers. There was a screened-in back porch. We had a small table on the back porch where we would eat our breakfast. We walked through this porch and onto the sidewalk to go from the house to the garage. Our clothesline was next to the sidewalk. The garage had a large front door for the car to enter and a small door in the rear. The back door faced the sidewalk and the clothesline.

One day I was walking on the sidewalk and as I passed the back garage door I looked in and saw my father lift Penny onto the hood of the car. His face was toward me and Penny's back was to me. He did not notice me. He kissed her in a way that a father should not kiss his daughter.

Penny remembers it this way: "daddy was mad at me for some reason, and it always bothered me to have him mad at me. I went to him in the garage where he was working to try to make up with him. He lifted me up onto the hood of the car. Then he said, 'Does this make you feel better?' He then kissed me and put his tongue in my mouth."

A short time later I stood under the clothesline and told my mother that daddy had kissed Penny in a wrong way. She told me that it was okay for a daddy to kiss his daughter, and that I was just being jealous of Penny. She told me that I had to stop being jealous of my sister.

Before Penny and I discussed this memory of hers, before any of these memories came back to me, I always had a bad feeling about the back door of that garage. Sometimes I would think about that door and that garage and I would have a feeling about a bad secret. It is hard to explain. Why would I ever even think about a garage door? Let alone a bad feeling about it?

Penny had another memory. We discussed it for the first time after she shared her feelings with me about her being molested. When she first talked with me about this memory it sounded familiar. In her memory she saw a tiny hand holding a penis. Then looking to her left she saw a little girl with blond hair in ringlets. This memory, she said, always confused her. She naturally believed that she must be the little girl but could not understand this memory. The hand and the little girl seemed to be in different places and not attached. Penny is the only daughter still with blond hair. One day we were looking at pictures from my picture album. She saw a little blond girl with ringlets in her hair. "That's her! That's the little girl I remember seeing."

I responded, "The little girl in the ringlets is me."

At a later time I said to her, "The little girl was wearing a yellow dress, wasn't she?"

Penny answered, "Yes, the dress was pale yellow, almost white. I never told a soul about this memory; I never even told Bob."

My Little Girl kept telling Penny.

I wasn't jealous of you. I tried to help. When he was with me he wouldn't be with you.

Did the Little Girl see her father with her sister? Did she try to protect her sister?

Later, I remembered the feeling I had when I saw his penis in Penny's hand. I remember the whole thing now.

I was about four years old. We lived in a small house across the street from Lake Huron and the Coast Guard Station. I looked in a bedroom through the doorway and saw Penny with our dad's penis in her hand. "Oh, no! Now I have to protect her, too," was the thought that came to my mind. It was a feeling of desolation and despair. I felt that it was more than I could handle.

CHAPTER 6

THE DREAM

There is one clear memory from my childhood that I do have. It has always been very vivid to me. When I was a little girl I was always afraid to go to bed because I was sure that I would have the dream again. And I did. Every night I had the same dream.

In my dream there had been a fire in our house and it had burned down. I never saw the fire in my dream, but I knew it had happened. It was evening. The firemen took us to the river and put us in the cold, dark river because of our burns. We were each in a little stall of our own. I was alone in the river with a wooden fence around me. In my mind I can still see this stall. I knew my family was close by. I could almost feel the presence of my sisters and parents, but I could not see them. I was so afraid of the cold, dark water.

I don't believe that I ever thought of this dream in the daytime. It was just before I went to bed that it came to my mind. I was too frightened to mention it to anyone. Maybe it wasn't a dream. Maybe I just thought about it every night as I went to bed.

After my memories began to return, I told this dream to Penny. She was shocked because as a child, she had a very similar dream of the black water. At our visit with Bonnie, we were even further astounded to learn of her dream of dark water.

I remember as a child going to the lake to swim with my mother and sisters. I always enjoyed the water. One day, I was too frightened of the water to go near it. I played with my beach toys next to the car as far away from the lake as possible. I have been frightened of water every since. Especially when it is evening and the water is dark.

December 13, 1992

I woke up shaking this morning. I dreamed the little girls had drowned. Each one of them was alone in the cold, black water. My first thought was that it was because they told.

CHAPTER 7

FEELINGS

December 29, 1992

I decided today to write down a few of my feelings. It helps me to write. I seem to understand better the thoughts and memories I am now having.

What seems so strange to me is what I don't remember. I don't remember being molested as a child. Penny has memories of it. I have feelings. I have these words and emotions coming from out of me at times. What are they? They are so confusing. I rock back and forth, and I cry like a child. I may be going insane.

I have no feelings for my father. I do not love him. I do not hate him. I do not like him. I do not remember ever having feelings for him. I did enjoy spending time with him and talking with him these past years that we have been living in Michigan. We discussed politics a lot. We always disagreed. It was satisfying for me to disagree with him.

I have spent a lot of time looking at pictures of myself as a child. I have one of me ice staking with my father. I must have been 12 or 13 years old. I always had a funny feeling when I looked at that picture. I could never understand my feelings about it. I remember that I did not want to skate with him. I did not want to take his hand. As a child I told my mother I did not want my father to touch me. She said that it would make my father feel bad if he knew I did not want to touch him. Even as an adult now, as I drive past that same park where we skated I can still see us, a young girl in a yellow coat skating with her father. There is a frown on the girl's face, a smile on her father's. I still feel that same sick feeling.

I never have felt that I was important. I can do things for other people, but I am not important enough to do things for myself. I hardly ever buy clothes for me. My children are teenagers, and I am wearing many of the same clothes I wore when they were in elementary school. My children are important. Dan is important, but I am not.

I like to buy purses. Clothing is too threatening to buy. I panic in a dress shop. Even as a young adult, Bonnie would go shopping with me and force me to buy clothes. As I write these words, tears come to my eyes. I am very emotional. Why is it so difficult for me to pick out and purchase clothing for myself? Just a few months ago Stephanie and Dan went shopping with me and forced me to buy a suit. I cried in the store. I cried while looking for the outfit, and I cried while trying it on. Purses and shoes are fun for me to buy. I love to buy them. In fact, when I plan a day to work on my memories, I go out and treat myself to something nice first. Usually it is a purse. Then I go to a spot on the lake where no one else comes and I spend hours working on my journal or reading self-help books.

I have no memories at this time of anything improper being done to me. I don't understand my emotions. The emotions of my Little Girl are what make me wonder if indeed something was done to me. The things she said and felt. They are very real to her.

I feel so confused. I do not understand what is going on in my mind. I feel like I am two people: one an angry, sad and frustrated Little Girl; and the other, the adult Norma who is trying to live a normal life rearing five teenagers.

CHAPTER 8

PICTURES AND MORE MEMORIES

December 31, 1992

Where do I begin today? I have been studying pictures of me as a very small child for about a week. I sit on my bed for hours at a time and stare at these pictures. It seems that they have a story to tell me. I must know the story! I cannot keep my eyes off three pictures. Two days ago I brought a photograph home from Penny's picture album. It was a picture of my mother with three little girls, my two sisters and me. In the picture, Penny is about two years old and being held in her mother's arms with Bonnie on one side of her and me on the other side. This picture has haunted me.

This morning, I felt sure that the Little Girl was coming back to talk. I was afraid to be alone. I called Penny and went over to her house. I cried all the way there.

The Little Girl talked to Penny for a while. I don't remember too much of what she and Penny talked about. I do remember the Little Girl telling her this:

He put his thing in Bonnie. He put his thing in Penny.

Penny asked her who?

The Little Girl said, *daddy did it.*

Penny said that she then called him names. Penny asked the Little Girl what he did to Norma. The Little Girl did not answer. Penny then asked, "Did he penetrate you?" The Little Girl was confused and would not answer.

"Did he touch you where he shouldn't?"

Yes.

I was crying very hard at this time. I was becoming very agitated. Penny was worried about me. She told me she was going to call her therapist and explained to him what was going on. We had talked to him as a family previously. I said that I did not want to be alone for very long so she asked Bob, her husband, to be with me in the bedroom while she made the phone call.

When Bob came in he hugged me and I started to cry on his shoulder. I showed him the picture of the three little girls, Bonnie, Norma and Penny. I said to him, "He did it to me when I was that size," pointing to Penny, "and I knew how bad it hurts, so I couldn't let him do it to her."

Penny came back into the room. Jeff, her therapist, had told her to be sure that I was aware of my surroundings. Then she could take me for a ride to clear my mind, or I could write. He said that I should choose. I said I wanted to write.

She brought me a small pad of paper and a pencil. I sat on the floor of her bedroom and then I started to write. I wrote very fast. As soon as I was finished with one page I tore it off and continued to write on the next page. I knew what I was writing, but I did not think about it. The words just seemed to flow from me. Suddenly it was over. I put the paper and pencil on the floor, and I was back to myself. I was always aware of what I was doing. I felt like someone else was writing and using my hand to put these feelings down on paper.

This is what the Little Girl wrote. I am writing it as she did. Spelling and punctuation are the same as she used.

Daddy did this to me! I hate daddy. My little sister -my big sister. He hurt them. I hate him. I tried to protect them - I couldn't I was to little to help. She wouldn't listen to me. I tried so hard. I had to protect my sisters. There was no one else. Aunt Norma didn't understand. I couldn't tell her. I was embarrassed. Penny was so little and Bonnie so weak. He didn't like me because I was so strong. I fought with him. I made a lot of noise. He was afraid Aunt Norma would hear. I beat him. Then I saw him with Bonnie and I had to try and stop it. - so I didn't fight it. It was so awful - but it was worth it - anything to protect Bonnie - then it started with Penny. We lived across the street from the lighthouse and Penny was so little. So I went to him so he wouldn't touch her again - but he did touch her again and over and over again and I couldn't stop it. I wanted to kill him - but I was too little to know how. But it would have stopped him forever. He deserved to die for making Bonnie and Penny cry. The angels help me be strong so I could protect my sisters. They helped me over and over again. I knew they were there to help me help them because we all had to live. We all had to live - we will get better but he won't.

What does all this mean? It seems like I have memories, and I don't know whose memories they are. I feel these memories are someone else, and are not a part of the adult Norma. I have a hurting Little Girl inside of me. How could

27

she hurt so badly, and I not be aware of it before. I don't understand any of this. Often I think I am going crazy. The emotions and memories of the Little Girl are so strong.

Sometime after this memory, I remembered that my parents had showed us the house we had lived in when my Uncle Lyle and Aunt Norma lived in the apartment above us. I was two or three years old at the time we were living there.

The written memory of the Little Girl was so difficult for me to understand. It seemed that the emotions were almost from another person. It has been difficult for me to comprehend that I am the Little Girl

(A note here about the above writings of the Little Girl: I later remembered all the things she wrote at that time. It took me over two years to do so, but every single thing she wrote was a memory I had to uncover.)

CHAPTER 9

TALKING TO DAD

January 1993

Dan and I feel that we need to discuss these memories with my father. Hopefully it will help me heal faster. We telephoned my mother to make arrangements to go to their home to talk with them.

When I am feeling strong, I do not show emotions. In fact I am sure that it looks like I am very cold about all of this. There is no in between for me. I have to be cold or I get extremely emotional. I was very strong today as we talked with him about the abuse of my sisters and the Little Girl.

He said, "I didn't do it. I have no memory of ever doing anything of the kind." We talked for quite a while. He continued to deny any wrong doing. He said that he had been sexually abused as a young boy by a man in the neighborhood. He said he had never told this to anyone ever before. My mother seemed surprised to hear this.

As strange as it may seem, the day was not a bad day and we stayed and had dinner with them. I was feeling no emotions that day. Very seldom do I have emotions and memories the same day. It seems when I need to be strong I can be.

CHAPTER 10

SHE IS NOT A BAD LITTLE GIRL!

January 3, 1993

I need to write these thoughts of the Little Girl today.

She is happy that the secret is coming out. She wants to forget and be happy. She doesn't hate her daddy anymore. She is just so sorry that it had to happen. She really did try to stop it. Nobody understood so she just did what she had to do, no matter what.

Aunt Norma loved her but she didn't understand. Mama wouldn't listen. She made her feel dirty and bad. But she wasn't bad. She just had to protect her sisters. Nobody else would.

She is not a bad Little Girl. She just wants someone to know that. She never wanted to be bad. She doesn't want to make anybody unhappy now. She just wants to be better.

January 14, 1993

This evening I went into my room and I cried and cried. I cried so hard that I could hardly breathe! I shook my head no, and I slapped by face with closed fists. Dan came in and stopped me from hitting myself.

"It wasn't her fault! It wasn't her fault! It wasn't her fault! You have to believe that," I screamed to Dan. "The Little Girl wasn't bad! It wasn't her fault." I cried and screamed and stamped my feet. I held my head with both hands as I felt that it was about to explode.

"Give me a pencil and paper and let me write or I'll go crazy," I screamed to Dan. He gave me paper and pencil, and I began to write. The pencil didn't work so I threw it. He handed me another one.

When I first started to write I was still very emotional. I cried very hard as I tried to write. Feelings of frustration and sadness overcame me. After I wrote the first line I paused and cried some more. After I wrote the second line the emotions were gone, and I was just writing. Following is the exact writing and punctuation the Little Girl used. The parenthesis is added for better understanding.

It wasn't her fault!. Mama saw it. She blamed the Little girl and the little girl finally cried. her mamma made her cry her daddy didn't. she could handle what daddy did but not what mama thought - mama said she was bad - she was dirty - but she wasn't dirty - she only had to protect her sisters - she loved her sisters - she loved her sisters so much no one else was there to do it she had to do it - she wanted help she cried for help - but nobody - not even grandma helped her - she would have killed him if she could - she thought about it over and over again - how could she do it - with a gun with a knife - how could she do it - she never figured a way - maybe it was good that she didn't but she wanted to.

When the writing was finished I was much calmer. As an adult I started to talk to Dan about what happened to the Little Girl.

He didn't do it to Bonnie very much. He seemed satisfied with me; I didn't cry. I hated him so much. I couldn't cry. (For some reason, it was important to the Little Girl that she was in control.) I let him do it to me but I was in control. But with Penny, I couldn't stop it. I hated him so much. I felt guilty because I let him do it to me. Down deep I knew that it was the only way I could keep him from my sisters, but I still felt guilty.

I'm so tired. She was always tired. She didn't sleep good at night. Her teachers said she was always tired. I don't remember not being tired.

This was the first time the Little Girl and the adult Norma started coming together. I was conscious of talking with her and for her.

CHAPTER 11

MAMA

January 15, 1993

I am feeling the Little Girl's feelings today. The Little Girl is confused. She doesn't know how to feel about her mama. She shouldn't love her. It would be bad to love her. It would be dirty to love her. I don't know why she feels this way about her mother. I just write down the feelings she has as I feel them.

She wants to cry. She is confused. She feels nothing for her daddy. She doesn't want to love her mama, but she is afraid that she does. Who is there to love her? She just wants someone to love her for her. Won't someone love her just because she is Norma.

She wants to care. She doesn't understand why nobody cares. She is so sad—she is always sad and nobody cares. The Little Girl wants to cry today.

Many times throughout my healing, the adult Norma felt the Little Girl's feelings. I have cried, "Won't somebody love me, just because I'm me. Please, someone love Norma," I would cry over and over again. These were feelings and emotions that had to come out. Wendy, my youngest daughter, came to me one day when she heard me crying in my room wanting someone to love me. It made her cry. She said, "Mama I love you! Don't you know that I love you?" I tried to explain to her that it was the Little Girl who was hurting and crying. I knew that I was loved. Not only by her but our whole family. The adult Norma knew she was loved. The Little girl still spent many hours crying for love.

CHAPTER 12

THE BEDROOM

January 20, 1993

My life has been calm for a little while. My oldest son, Jared, has been preparing to leave for a two-year mission for our church and will be soon leaving for Korea.

I have been trying very hard for nothing to go wrong. I do not want Jared to be upset before he leaves for his mission. I have tried not to have any memories. When I did have them I did not record them. When I record my memories, it seems that I become much more emotional.

Jared wanted to spend some time with his grandparents because he would not be seeing them again for two years. It was very difficult for me, but I usually went with him while he visited them. We would spend time with them and then we would shop or have lunch before coming home. Occasionally he would go into a store for something on the way home while I waited in the car. As soon as he got out of the car I would burst into tears and sob. Then when I saw him come out of the store, I would wipe my face and be smiling by the time he got to the car. I don't know where I got the strength during those trying days to hide my emotions. It was very important to me that he could leave without worrying about me, and that he would be able to spend time with his grandparents.

February 7, 1993

Jared has left for his mission, and now I am ready to get on with my healing.

My children are aware of my repressed memories, but none of them know what the memories are about. They do not want to know now, so I respect their wishes. Perhaps someday they will want to know. They see my pain. They are not ready for more. They are all in high school except Jared who is on his mission. It is not fair for them to know all of this.

I have begun to see a therapist. She is very helpful to me while I am trying to cope with my life today as well as work on my memories. In my last session with her, she told me to ask the Little Girl questions when I have memories.

This evening I was sitting in my bedroom on the chair beside my bed. I started to rock back and forth. I rocked as though I was rocking a baby in my arms. I think that the Little Girl needs to be rocked, as I always seem to rock when she talks to me or I have memories of her.

I cried and cried. I covered my face with my hands, and I began to scream. I use the word scream because that is what I did. I screamed as though I were terrified for my life. The screaming turned to sobs as I buried by face in my hands. Finally the Little Girl began to speak. The following are her words.

I was in the little bedroom. My dad was lying on the floor— on his back. He had his clothes on.

I asked the Little Girl, "Where is Bonnie?"

She's at school.

"Where is Penny?"

She is hiding downstairs. She always hides.

"Where is your mother?"

She is in the kitchen listening to the radio—the black radio.

"What color is the room?"

I think it is blue. I can't remember the floor. I don't remember carpet. I don't think it was hard.

"Did mama see?"

The Little Girl wouldn't answer. The adult Norma did not want her to answer.

I was so tired after this conversation. I sat for a while in my chair beside my bed. I was rocking. The chair was not a rocking chair. I just rocked back and forth.

At last I stood up and went to my bed. I fell onto the bed and hugged my pillows. It is hard to explain my actions here. I was a frightened Little Girl trying to get comfort from her pillows. I curled up in a ball, hugging my pillow. I laid on my right side with my left leg moving up and down as though I were rocking myself to sleep. This soothed me like my rocking does when I am sitting up having memories.

My hands and arms stopped moving and I was peaceful and then asleep. I felt myself fall asleep.

Dan was sitting beside me during this conversation between Norma and the Little Girl.

February 11, 1993

I sat on my bed and rocked again today. I rocked and rocked for a long time.

I saw my dad on the floor again. I saw no bed, no dresser, no furniture at all, just my dad in a blue room. I still don't remember what's on the floor.

The Little Girl talked to Dan.

I'm so afraid of water. The cold lake—the bathtub. I can't breathe under water. I would die if I couldn't breathe. He would hold my head under and not let me up. I don't want to die. Who would protect my sisters? It would be easier if I did though.

He lay on the floor and said, "You know what I like you to do."

I don't like to do it.

He said, "You do it and don't make any noise or I will find Penny. I know where she is hiding. She thinks I don't know where she is hiding, but I do."

I'm too big for this daddy. I don't want to do it.

I didn't want the Little Girl to tell me what I did. I have been afraid of this all along. The Little Girl felt guilty because she went to him to help her sisters.

I think that this is an older girl I am remembering in this memory.

CHAPTER 13

DID IT REALLY HAPPEN?

February 12, 1993

As an adult, since my repressed memories and emotions have been returning, I have not understood my feelings toward my mother. I don't want to hurt her. I don't want to be with her. I don't want to talk with her about it.

I watched LaToya Jackson on TV today. She was discussing her abuse as a child and the denial of her family. Somehow, hearing her made me feel stronger.

I realized that I did not want to confront my mother about her knowing because I was afraid that she would deny any previous knowledge of it. Then she would believe him instead of believing me. I felt that she had to believe me. If not it would make me doubt the reality of it. She had finally told me that she believed me that he molested me. She had no idea that I had memories of her knowing about it. She has said over and over again, "If only I knew I would have stopped it. Why didn't you tell me?"

Whenever she said that to me, I would get very upset. I felt like the Little Girl was to blame for all that happened. Then the guilt feelings all came back.

It doesn't matter anymore what she thinks. Even if she doesn't remember or believe me, I know it happened! It makes no difference what she knew, or remembered or saw. The fact is that it did happen and she did know it.

The Little Girl was always positive that her mother knew what was occurring. The first thing that came out of her mouth when she spoke was:

She knew, she knew, I told her, she knew.

Every time the Little Girl speaks she tells me her mother knew. Her mother told her she was jealous of Penny. The Little Girl knew all along her mama knew. But this was a very difficult thing for the adult Norma to face.

February 12, 1993

I am very despondent today. I am going to journal my thoughts.

I'm worthless—I want to get in the bathtub and go under and not get up. It would be so much easier. I want to beat myself. Pull my hair. Hurt me. I must hurt me!

My mother never cared. I still feel like nobody cares. I carry it alone. I'm always alone. I want to be alone. I want nobody around me. I don't want to share this with anyone. I just want to go away—all alone!

The adult Norma was feeling the feelings of the Little Girl, only she was feeling them as an adult. The adult Norma knows that she has people who love her and share her pain, but she, at times, still feels this loneliness that the Little Girl feels.

I slept on the floor tonight beside my bed because I had to be alone. I pretended I was sleeping when Dan came in to go to bed.

After all this time, I still wonder occasionally if it is real. It cannot be real. These things don't happen!

CHAPTER 14

A QUIET DAY

February 13, 1993

Dan and I stayed home today. It was quiet all day. The kids have gone to a basketball game and then to a church activity.

I slept on the floor last night. I know that Dan worried about it. Today has been a most unusual day. Dan is always busy doing something. He can't sit still. I was so tired I stayed in bed all day. Dan never left my side. I know that it must have been hard for him to do. I kept telling him that he did not need to stay with me. He just sat in the chair next to the bed and said, "This is where I want to be."

It has been a very important day for me. First, I realized, once again, how much support Dan gives to me. Second, it has given me the opportunity to rest my mind.

Later that night we went with the kids to a church dance about 60 miles away. They went in one car and Dan and I drove alone in our other car. Coming home Dan and I began to talk.

I finally realized, or could admit, what bothers me most about my parents' attitude concerning my memories. It is their preoccupation with what my memories are doing to them. I have never felt that they thought about me, what I am going through. Instead it is how this affects them. What would people say? What will it do to their marriage? I kept looking for what they felt for me. I wanted to be comforted by them. They could not give this to me.

Once I recognized this, it freed me. I can stop worrying about them. Stop worrying about what my memories are doing to them and begin to concentrate on my own healing, no matter what the consequences.

It is easy here to write that I should stop worrying about them. It is much easier to write than to do. I decided not to worry about them, but my thoughts were always, how do they feel? Am I hurting them by staying away? Were my memories hurting them?

CHAPTER 15

TELLING MOM

February 15, 1993

Monday morning. The kids were home from school for the day. I had made plans to do things with them. We had to get Stephanie's college loan papers mailed out. Then we were going shopping for formals for the girls. I was looking forward to spending the day with my daughters.

The phone rang. It was Penny. She said mom wanted to know if I could perm her hair today. Mom told Penny we could do it at Penny's house so I would not have to see my dad. Mom has no idea of my frustrating feelings toward her.

All of my excitement for the day left me. I told Penny that I could do mom's hair later in the day, after everything else was done.

The first part of the day was enjoyable for me. We completed Stephanie's paperwork, and we found a beautiful dress for Wendy. We had lunch and went home.

About 2:00 I began to cry. At first it was a soft cry, but I could not stop. As the afternoon wore on I cried harder and harder. By 4:00 I was close to hysterics. I sobbed and sobbed. I could not stop crying. I couldn't even think straight.

"I can't go!" I told Dan.

"I'm glad you made that decision," Dan replied. He has never forced me in any of my dealings with my emotions. "I will call her for you," he said.

I told him I wanted her to know why I couldn't come. I wanted her to know that the Little Girl believed that she knew what was going on and that she didn't stop it. I had to have that secret out. I couldn't pretend any longer. I wasn't strong enough to tell her myself. I couldn't even be there when Dan told her. I knew it was the coward's way out. I worried over my sanity today. I am afraid I will go over the edge today.

Dan went to Penny's house to talk to mom. Penny and Bob were there also. She became very angry when he told them about the Little Girl and her understandings. I don't know how much they understand about the Little Girl. She confuses anyone I talk to about her. Mom grabbed her purse to go home.

Dan said, "I will leave. You stay here with Penny."

It was a great relief for me to know that mom knew how the Little Girl felt. I am sure mom feels she will never see me again. I don't know.

Later that evening I began to think about going to my parents' home. It seemed that a load had been lifted from me because I no longer had to pretend. It has just been too hard to pretend. I now felt like I could talk to them.

February 16, 1993

I want to go see my parents today. I'm sure yesterday was very hard for them. I don't think we should call first. I can't feel pressure if I decide at the last minute I can't go through with it. I know I am being selfish. I just have to do it this way.

Dan and I drove along the St. Clair River to my parents' home. As I was watching the river I talked to my Little Girl. I told her where we were going and that we were going to talk about our childhood. I told her if there was anything she wanted to say to either of them it was okay with me.

We arrived at my parents' home about 2:30 in the afternoon. My mother was very surprised and pleased to see us. My dad was in the living room. I didn't say anything to him.

I told my mother I wanted to talk with her. We sat down at the kitchen table and began to converse.

I tried to explain to her that the Little Girl believed that her mother was aware of what was going on. I also tried to explain that she was a Little Girl and perhaps misunderstood. As an adult, I just had the emotions of my Little Girl who felt strongly about it.

I heard my father in the living room begin to cry. I got up and went in to him. He was sitting in his chair. As I stood in front of him, he said, "I have never been so hurt in my life."

I told him that he had hurt me as a child. I was very calm at this time.

He said that he had never touched me.

The Little Girl emerged! She screamed at the top of her lungs:

I was three years old and you raped me!

I don't remember what else she said.

(When this happened I believed it was my little three-year-old girl who said this. Now, I don't believe it was my Little Girl who emerged here. Later in my memories I heard from older girls who were part of my repressed memories. I think this was my 14-year-old girl speaking. It sounds more like her. You will learn more of her later in the book.)

My mother left the room in tears. Dan followed her and said, "Let them alone. They need to talk."

Later Dan told me that we screamed at each other for a while. I only remember a little of it.

I turned around to leave and my father said, "Let me tell you something!" I turned back to him and said, "Okay, talk!"

Then we started to speak in normal conversational manner. The screaming was over. Dad said he didn't understand the Little Girl. He said, "You don't remember anything yourself. It's just what the Little Girl tells you."

I told him that I remember when I was three years old, when I was five years old, and when I was twelve years old.

This was the Little Girl speaking using the adult Norma's voice. The adult Norma did not remember these things at this time. The words just came out of her mouth. It was the same as at the restaurant with my sisters.

He seemed surprised at this statement.

I had previously talked with him about his lack of emotions for my feelings and what I was going through. I told him that a friend I had confided in had told her husband. Her husband put his head on the table and cried. He cried for me. He cared enough to cry for me. My father cried for himself.

My father asked, "You have talked to people about this?" I told him I needed to be able to talk to someone. No one I spoke to knew him or my family. He said he needed to talk to someone. I suggested he talk to his minister or a therapist.

His reply was, "If I talked to anyone about this, your mother would leave me."

I assured him she would not leave him. I had already told her what he did, and she was still with him.

My father and I seemed freer and more at ease with each other. That was the last time I saw my parents for a couple of weeks. It is still difficult to spend time with them.

CHAPTER 16

LITTLE NORMA TALKS TO DAN

February 25, 1993

I cannot sleep at night. I need to talk with the Little Girl, but I cannot force the situation. It is her decision to talk with me. My therapist said that perhaps she is tired from the emotional outlet with my father. She may not be sure about the adult relationship with her mother either. Where does it leave her?

March 6, 1993

I have not been sleeping well. I stay awake most nights. About 10:00 this evening I was reading out loud to Dan. What I was reading was very close to me, and I was emotional. He went to sleep!

When I saw him sleeping, I was a little girl, all alone again. I cried and cried.

Dan woke up, and we talked for a long time. I knew the Little Girl wanted to talk to me but she seemed self conscious.

Finally the Little Girl said:

I'm 13 years old. I'm so alone. Penny has friends. Bonnie has friends. My cousins don't like me. They are boys. I'm alone at Grandma's. Penny has everything I wanted. I really am not jealous of Penny. Judy was my friend, but we never had fun. She likes me because nobody else did. We were alike. She took care of her brothers. I protected my sisters. We are like two old ladies. Why am I taking care of Penny? She should be taking care of herself. Am I doing it because I want to?

Dan asked, "Does your mother give you attention?"

No.

"Does your father give you attention any other way?"

No.

The Little Girl stopped talking. Dan said, "Come again when you are ready. I want to talk to you some more."

Do you really mean that?

"Yes," said Dan. The Little Girl continued to talk to Dan. Dan asked her if she was still 13 years old. The Little Girl did not answer the question, but continued:

He was lying on the floor. He had me unzip his pants. I didn't want to do it. Then that thing came out. He made me touch it. I didn't like to touch it. He said it felt good.

Mother came in. He was surprised. She was mad and sent me to my room. I was happy now because it was going to stop. I lay on my bed. I felt safe there. Then she came in and yelled at me! Why was she yelling at me? She called me names."

Dan asked, "What names?"

Dirty, ugly, bad. She was mad at me!! I wanted to die. It would be so much better if I died. She made me promise to never do it again.

Dan asked, "Did she holler at him?"

I don't know. I think so. He said he would never do it again if she wouldn't tell anyone. But it didn't stop it. She was in the kitchen with her radio on. I hated that radio. I wanted to smash it with a hammer. My dad never liked me. Now my mother doesn't like me either.

As the Little Girl told this story to Dan there was not a lot of emotion in it. Later, on another day, my emotions came. It seems I can't handle emotions and memories at the same time so they often come separately.

I believe that this was the memory of my four-year-old, not my thirteen-year-old. I am not sure why my thirteen-year-old appeared this day. It is the only time so far that she has spoken to me.

CHAPTER 17

MEMORIES OF THE ACT

March 11, 1993

I was home alone today. I relaxed in the tub. It seemed to help me. Water is strange for me. It either scares me to death or soothes me completely. I don't understand it.

As I lay in the tub I asked myself, "What did he do to you?" Then I knew I needed to ask my Little Girl, but did not want to: "What did you do to him?"

He was lying on the floor facing up. I can't remember the floor. The room was blue. He had his clothes on. I saw his face. He was young. He had brown hair. He was thin.

He was lying on the floor facing up. I was beside him at about his waist. My feet were under me, my toes outstretched. I was sitting on my legs. I would have to lean up and off my legs to reach him. I had to unzip his pants, and take his thing out. I would have to hold it in my hand, moving my hand a few times. Then I had to put it in my mouth. Then he would groan, "That feels so good, Norma. You like it don't you? I know you do or you wouldn't do it for your dad."

I hated it so much, but I didn't tell him. When I did this to him he forgot about Penny. I thought he did anyway. The Little Girl didn't cry. Her eyes would get red. She just walked out of the room after her daddy left. She went to her room and picked up a doll, a little doll with no hair and a pink outfit. She sat on her bed and hugged and hugged her doll.

The adult Norma cried at the sight of this. I still cry when I remember the Little Girl sitting on her bed, hugging her doll.

Oh mama, how could you blame that little girl? I'm so sad for the Little Girl. How could you blame her? She walked right past the kitchen door to her bedroom. You were baking bread and had the radio on. That stupid, awful radio.

Later as I recorded this memory, I shut my eyes and saw me. I could see me in different ages. We were all in one picture. I saw a tall me with curly hair, I saw a little me with blond curly hair to my shoulders. There was another one of me very small.

There were more memories to come...

While I was still in the tub, I asked, "What did he do to you?"

I laid on the floor with no clothes on. He rubbed my tummy. He rubbed the outside of my leg. Then he went higher on my tummy. Then he rubbed the inside of my leg. One of his hands was on my breast. Then his finger went inside of me, rubbing my breast with the other hand. Then my father said, "Doesn't this feel good, Norma?" He took his finger out of me and unzipped his pants and took the thing out. He put it where his finger had been. Then he went up and down and up and down. Finally he went down harder and stopped. Then he got up and he had a white towel. It had been there all along! He wiped himself off with it, and then he wiped the floor. He told me to get dressed, and he was going to the barn. I slowly got dressed and walked with my head down into the bedroom and played with my paper dolls.

CHAPTER 18

I CAN'T BREATHE!

March 12, 1993

Last night I discussed all my memories with Dan. I cried a lot. Then we talked some more, and I started to rock again. I cried so hard it was literally difficult for me to breathe.

"I can't breathe! I don't want to drown!" I felt terror. I have never, in my memory, felt terror as I did at that moment.

I was sitting on the chair beside my bed, and I dove onto the bed screaming, "I'll never do it again, I promise!"

Then I felt Dan next to me. I grabbed him around the neck. I felt safe, relieved. I held him very tightly as I cried and cried.

I began hyperventilating again. I remember thinking, "You have to calm down, Norma." I started to breathe deeply and settled down. Then I left Dan's arms, and I sat in my chair. I started to rock again. I rocked for quite awhile, and then I said in a different voice:

You're just like the rest of them.

I sat quiet for a while with my hands over my eyes. Then I was back to normal. My eyes are always shut tight with my hands over them when I have memories.

I never did figure out what, "You're just like the rest of them" meant. Dan said I sounded just like my mother when I said it.

March 13, 1993

This morning I woke up a 5:00 completely exhausted. My eyes hurt so badly that I could hardly keep them open. I went back to bed after everyone left. I slept soundly for a couple of hours. When I woke up, my whole body hurt. It hurt for the rest of the day.

CHAPTER 19

THE ANGELS

March 14, 1993

Sunday morning. I was too emotional to go to church with my family today. I received a letter from Dan's mother two days ago. In her letter she blamed me for some things I had no control over. I couldn't understand why she wrote such a letter to me. It was so out of character for her. It was more than I could handle. I was blamed again, only this time by a different mother!

About 1:15, I got into the bathtub. I was reading a book. All of a sudden I had a strong feeling to roll over in the tub. It wasn't the adult Norma needing to roll over. It was a peaceful feeling just to roll over. I mentally and physically shook my head. "Don't be silly Norma."

Again, I had this strong, peaceful feeling. Roll over. "Okay," I said out loud, "Let the memories come."

The memories unfolded as follows:

I was in the bathtub, lying on my stomach—motionless. I watched myself this way for awhile. I saw me. I was about four years old. I was small enough to lie completely in the bathtub head to toe. I was on my stomach. I was not moving. I saw my blond hair, wet, down to my shoulders.

I felt arms under my waist and me being lifted out of the water. I could feel the heavy weight of my body as my head and my feet hung lower than my waist.

The adult Norma, watching this scene, asked, "Who are they? Who are these people? There are two of them. They are not mom. Not dad. Not Bonnie. I could not figure out who they were. They were not anyone I knew. They were adults. I did not recognize their faces. I still do not remember what their faces looked like. They were dressed in white. I was not frightened of them. They were kind and gentle. We were still in the bathroom when one of them began to talk to me. She sat on the edge of the bathtub and held me in her arms. She had wrapped a towel around me and said, "You must never do that again, Norma. You have a Father in Heaven who loves you very much. We love you very much. You are here for a very special reason, and you must take care of yourself. We will help you."

I seemed to sense that they were very special people. I don't remember all they said to me. I remember asking them, "Will you stay with me?"

The woman answered, "We will be here when you need us. You likely won't see us, but we will always be near." The woman held me in her arms and rocked me. She rocked me for a long time. I felt warmth and love as my eyes closed. As the scene of the child self being rocked disappeared I saw a beautiful bright pink light. The color was warm and divine. It stayed with me for a long time.

CHAPTER 20

SELF DESTRUCTION

March 28, 1993

Yesterday and today were very busy, hectic days. Dan and I came home after being gone most of the weekend. I was in tears by the time Dan drove our car into the driveway. I felt very self destructive. The adult Norma felt this way. I hurried into the house and locked myself in my bedroom.

I have to hurt me! I have to end it! I started to slap my face with my fists, and I stomped my feet. My head was so full of emotions.

Memories...

I was fighting him. Kicking him, making noise. He told me to shut up. I didn't. He hit me on the face. I don't think it was a very hard hit. He left me. He was afraid Aunt Norma, who lived in the apartment above us, would hear me.

He went to Bonnie. I looked in and saw him with her. She was crying. When I saw her crying I was devastated. I knew that it was my fault that she was crying.

It's my fault, it's my fault. It's my fault! It's my fault! I beat on my pillow. If I hadn't fought with him he wouldn't have gone to her. I continued to beat my pillow with my fist. I felt such despair. It was my fault he did this to Bonnie. Bonnie had had polio and was not very strong. I was supposed to take care of her. It was my fault that she was hurt.

I cried for a long time that it was my fault. I was so little. I don't know how I understood all that was going on. I felt responsible for her. It was my fault that Bonnie was crying.

I knew at the moment I saw him with Bonnie that I could never let it happen again. I knew in my heart that I had to be the protector of my sister. I would do whatever was necessary to keep him away from her regardless of the consequence to me.

Dan said, "It wasn't your fault, Norma. You were a child. How could you protect your sister from a man? How could you have stopped him?"

I still felt that it was my fault.

CHAPTER 21

DENIAL

April 2, 1993

Penny was out of town for a week, and when she came home she called me to ask what happened with mom and dad. I told her that I had not seen them.

She said that mom and dad were both upset about all of this. Dad had been crying and wanted to go into a psychiatric ward at the hospital.

I felt so badly about what I was putting them through that I started to wonder if it really had occurred. It couldn't have happened. We were a happy family and nothing like that could have transpired.

For two weeks I felt terrible guilt for hurting them. I kept saying to myself that it could not have happened. During those two weeks I hardly slept. I cried most of the time. I could not leave my bedroom. I would make a sandwich and hurry back to my room to eat it. It was the only place I felt safe.

I felt self destructive. I wanted to hurt myself. I felt intense anger. I felt terrible guilt. During my session with my therapist, I realized that I was in denial again. I don't want it to have happened; therefore, I needed to believe that it didn't.

My mind would not allow this denial to go on.

I have decided to write out my thoughts and feelings of my abuse, and then study them so that I could know for sure what really happened to me.

My options:

1. I am making up my memories for attention or for some other reason.

2. I am going insane and have no control over my life or anything else.

3. I was sexually, emotionally and physically abused as a child; and my parents have either forgotten it, or blocked it out for emotional reasons, or are lying about it now.

None of these options are easy. They all hurt. I can't decide which I want to be true. I have to know what is true. The choice of what is true is not mine to make but mine to discover.

Now I must analyze my choices.

1. If I am making this up, I must have a reason. The only reason I can think of would be for attention. If I am doing it for attention: Do I want attention so badly that I will hurt that much for it? When the memories return the hurt is so intense.

2. Why do I have them when I am alone? Sometimes I cry so hard and hurt so badly when no one is around.

3. Am I so selfish that I would put Dan through this trauma so that he will hold me in his arms when he is happy to hold me anytime?

4. Am I so insecure that I will do anything to get people to notice me?

5. Am I going insane? I have normal times when I can function as an adult. I can control my emotions to protect my children. I can spend quality time with my children and discuss deep things with them. I do have times when I feel that I am not stable. Writing helps me to calm down.

6. Did my parents abuse me? If so, my mother can't face the fact that it happened, and she was aware of it, so she has mentally blocked it out. In so doing she is hurt because of what I am saying. Or she remembers it, but will never admit it because it is easier to lie and deny it than to say, "Yes, it happened. I should have stopped it. I had no idea it would affect you so much, even later in life."

   Was my father a different personality when it happened and so has no remembrance and no responsibility; thus no consequence for him. Or, he remembers and denies it all because it is easier for him than to say, "I did it. I'm sorry. I had no idea the emotional effect it would have on you."

Now that I have written my thoughts down I can think them over calmly, without so much emotion that I get confused. If it did happen, what my parents remember or do not remember does not change the fact that it happened.

April 14, 1993

I have come to the conclusion that it really did occur. These two weeks have been pretty uneventful; really pretty good.

CHAPTER 22

BACK TO NORMAL—FOR A WHILE ANYWAY

May 19, 1993

I have had no memories or emotions of the Little Girl returning for awhile. I have been trying to get on with my life, as well as understand my feelings and emotions as an adult.

I continue to read books to help me understand what is going on inside of me. Sometimes I cry as I study them because I see me in them. Writing has always been helpful to me so I have kept a journal of my daily emotions.

I do not love myself now. I do not hate me. I just have no self love. I want to hurt my father. I feel like I will be better if he hurts. I want to run away from life, all of life. I am very bitter.

Did I say back to normal? I guess I'm really not ready to say normal. I realize that I need help in letting go of my anger. Sometimes I have no desire to get better. I just want to die and have it over with. I am afraid to be happy. If I feel myself smiling or being happy I force it away. I don't understand why.

I am afraid Dan will abandon me. I am afraid to love him. I have been hurt by people who were supposed to love me.

I feel dirty when I think of my mother. I feel it would be dirty to love her. Perhaps it is because he talked about her while molesting me.

May 22, 1993

Father's Day is coming up. What will I do? We went out of town on Mother's Day. Our whole family went to my parents' home on Saturday to give my mother a present. That way I didn't have to worry about Mother's Day. What will I do for Father's Day?

I have been upset with Penny. She knew that she had been molested. She has dealt with it in her own way. I am happy for her. But she wants me to pretend it never happened. Perhaps she can do that. Perhaps in time I will be able to do that. I cannot now. It is too real to me.

May 25, 1993

I know what I want. I want someone to be outraged at what happened to me. I want them to be angry. I don't want to keep it a secret anymore. I am angry and I want to be angry.

I want my sisters to appreciate what I did for them. I want them to know, to really know, what I went through for them. I want them to say thank you. I want my mother to say, "You poor thing. I am so sorry that happened to you!" I want to be comforted by my mother and my sisters.

I want my father to hurt like he hurt me. I want to holler at him. I want to tell him how I really feel about him. Then I want him out of my life.

May 30, 1993

I need distance from my family. Penny has gone into denial. She says if it happened it was long ago. She doesn't want to remember it anymore. She says, "If daddy did anything to me, I forgive him. He doesn't remember anything." When she and my mother and father deny it, or act like it never happened, even if they do believe me, it hinders my recovery. I cannot act as though it never happened. Even Bonnie hinders me in some ways. I am so pleased to have Dan and a few friends to believe me, or I may go crazy.

I still have emotions built up inside of me, especially with my mother. I have a need to cry hard. Why do I have more anger towards my mother than my father?

I always wanted to be an actress. I wanted to act out emotions. My mother always told me not to cry. When my dog, Chris, was hit by a car and died, she said that I needed to be grateful it wasn't a child. I wanted to cry for Chris. I cried today for Chris. Twenty-eight years later I cried. I feel better.

I think I am so angry with my mother because I could never be free with her. I always had to hide the real me.

I feel like I need to tell my story. No one wants to hear it, but I must tell it.

As I have written my feelings in this chapter I hope that it will help others as it has helped me by putting them down on paper. I am not alone. You are not alone. It helps to know that we are not alone.

CHAPTER 23

GETTING BETTER

June 18, 1993

I am staying away from my parents, and I am doing much better. I am not nearly so bitter and angry. I realized that I had to let these feelings be a part of me so that I could feel them and then let them go.

I can remember things that have happened in the past, and be angry over them. But it does not affect my life today. I can feel the anger and then let it go. I no longer feel guilt for feeling anger. To me that is a huge step towards healing.

Last New Year's Day was very difficult for me. I held in anger about that day for six months. I am not angry any more.

New Year's Day has always been one of our favorite family holidays. We eat junk food while we watch the Rose Parade and the Rose Bowl game. Just as the game was getting started, I received a phone call from my mother. My father was sick. She had to take him to the hospital, and she wanted me to go with her. At that time Penny was still having problems dealing with her memories and refused to see him. I had had enough memories to be confused about everything, but I was still strong enough to deal with my parents.

Dan and I left immediately. We spent the rest of the evening at the hospital with him. His penis had been bleeding caused by radiation treatments years before. The doctors were trying to get the bleeding under control.

The Little Girl and I had some very colorful discussions about his illness that night. We both decided that the best cure would be to cut it off. That would cure it in more ways than one.

The Little Girl and I are becoming closer. We need to be one. I think of us as one most of the time.

When my sisters realized that I believed our Mother knew of the abuse, they started to draw away from me. I never blamed my mother for the abuse. I still do not blame her, but I cannot deny the feelings of my Little Girl.

I feel like I have lost so much this past year. One great loss I feel is the loss of my sisters. Finally, though, I am okay with this. It has taken me a long time to be okay with this loss. They don't know how to deal with me. I still love them as I love my parents, but for healing purposes it is necessary for me to stay away from my family now.

My parents and my sisters have become very close through this. I must admit at times it makes me jealous. I sometimes feel hurt and sorry for myself as they draw closer to each other, and I just hurt more. I am grateful, though, that they have been able to draw strength from each other. I am pleased with their closeness. I have not always been able to say that.

As my healing progresses I have the ability to understand not only myself better, but also the rest of my family.

CHAPTER 24

THE WORST DAY OF MY LIFE

June 28, 1993

I talked with the Little Girl today. I told her that I wanted to remember all that happened on the day that my mother came in, the emotions and the memories. I need to know. She needed to tell me. I told her I loved her and that it was all right to talk about it.

The Little Girl began to talk to me.

> *I was four years old. It started out like many other times. He came in from the barn. He had me go into the room with him. I didn't want to, but I did. He lay on the floor and had me unzip his pants. They smelled of oil. He was lying on the floor. I was on my knees beside him. His thing was in my hand. I was moving it up and down. I started to lean over to put it in my mouth. I felt sick to my stomach.*

> *She came in. She had on a yellow dress. Her hair was short. She was so surprised and so mad. She said, "Go to your room, Norma." I felt happy. Mother really knew now. She would never let it happen again. I left and went and sat on my bed. The bedroom was blue. I was nervous.*

> *I heard him say, "I'm sorry, Marguerite. I'll never do it again. Please don't tell anybody. I could go to jail."*

> *"You dirty bastard. You deserve to be in jail."*

"No, Marguerite, please no."

I don't want to hear anymore. I laid down on the bed and waited for her to come in. She comes in. I think she will hug me. She doesn't hug me. She hit me! She hit me on the face. I'm screaming, "I'm sorry, mama, I'll never do it again. Please don't hit me again."

I'm so scared I can't breathe. I don't know what she is going to do. She left the room. I'm all alone. She hates me now. Why does she hate me? It wasn't my fault. I only wanted to help. I had to protect Bonnie. She told me to take care of Bonnie. I had to protect Penny. Why wouldn't she help me? Oh, please, somebody help me.

She tells me to take a bath. I'm so dirty. Nothing will clean me. But I need a bath. I think she wants me to die. I'm so afraid of water. She is running the water in the tub for me! The sound of running water terrified me. I hate her. I hate her more than I hate him. Maybe they will find me dead and blame her. She would deserve that.

I lay in the tub. I feel so good. Roll over Norma, nothing to be afraid of. Roll over. So peaceful— nobody can hurt you again. Roll over. It's so peaceful. I should have done this sooner. Why didn't I do this sooner? Good bye mama.

As I remembered, and as I wrote this last paragraph I felt so peaceful. The trauma of the other memories was gone, and I felt at peace with dying.

My angels literally saved me that day. Then they gave me the love and hugs I wanted and needed so badly. They have been with me throughout my life.

As I have remembered and pondered this experience I have noted the emotional rollercoaster ride that the Little Girl experienced the day her mama came in and saw her with her daddy. I must write it down here.

Her father came to her and the Little Girl felt:

- Anger   I hated him so much.
- Just blah   Nothing I could do about it. Just endure it.

Her mother came in and she felt:

- Scared   Just for a moment.
- Happy   It would be over. She won't let it happen again.
- Relief   I don't have to be scared anymore.

Her mother sent her to her room. Then she felt:

- Relief   I am glad to be out of the room.
- Nervous/
  Excitement   I waited for her to come in and hug me.
- Just Nervous   She stays and talks with him and does not come to me right away.
- Surprised   She comes in and yells at me. She calls me a dirty little bad girl.
- Scared   She has a look on her face. She hits me. She hollers at me, more than at him. Why?
- Confused   Why is she blaming me? She said, "You're just like the rest of them." Who, mama, who?

- Anger   It's not my fault! You should help me.
- Scared   She hits me and then leaves me. I'm all alone. I am only safe when I am alone.
- Peace   I decide to die.

September 28, 1993

As I was rereading my journal today, I stopped and cried. I still only feel safe when I am alone. Many times I do not want Dan or my children near me. I only feel safe and secure when I am alone.

CHAPTER 25

SUICIDAL THOUGHTS

January 4, 1994

I think I am getting better, then a few months go by and I learn that I have much more to do.

I am thinking of visiting my parents today. I need them. I need them to comfort me. I need them to hold me. I know they can't, but I have to try. I have to do this alone, without Dan. I must handle my memories on my own.

Dan cannot help me. I called him at work today. I told him that I loved him and that I was sorry. I was crying. I hung up. He called me back and said he would come right home. I told him no, I did not want him to come home.

I felt a need to die. I got into the car and I started to drive. I drove into town and to my parent's home. I parked on the street so that I had no chance of being blocked in the driveway. I needed to feel safe in the knowledge that I could leave whenever I wanted to.

I walked into the house. My mother met me at the door. "I want to die." I sobbed this to my mother. She rushed to the phone to call Penny. "Don't call Penny!" I wanted her to hold me, not to call Penny.

It was a trying ordeal for my parents. They didn't know how to handle me. They kept wanting to call someone. I knew they were worried about me, but I didn't care. I wasn't even sure why I was there. I wanted something from them. I really didn't know what. I did want to die.

I sat on the floor in their living room, put my head on the couch and cried. I said to my father, "You really don't remember doing anything to me?"

He answered me, "No."

I threw the cushions off the couch and across the room. I sobbed and sobbed. Every time my mother tried to call Penny, I screamed at her, "Don't call Penny!"

I am sure my parents thought that I had gone mad. When I had calmed down a bit my father asked me, "Does this happen often, Norma?" I told him, "Yes, I have lived through almost two years of hell."

I then told them that I was leaving. I put my coat on and walked to the door. I told them that I loved them and that I was sorry for the pain I had caused them. I told them that we would never speak of this again. At that moment I did not know if I would ever see them again. I still wanted to die. I then turned and walked to my car with my head held high. Somehow I felt released.

It took me months to figure out what I wanted from my parents that day. I guess I cannot blame them for not knowing my need, when even I did not know. The adult Norma and the Little Girl Norma wanted to be comforted. We both wanted to be cried with and held. We both wanted to be told, "I am so sorry for your pain."

The release I felt when I left that day was the knowledge that they will never be able to give me what I need from them. I know it now, so I must let go.

I spent some time driving along the lake and then I went home. When I got home, I had my daughter, Wendy, call them to tell them I was home and that I was all right. I didn't want them to worry about me.

Later I learned that as soon as I left, my mother called Penny and then Penny called Dan. They were all angry with Dan for years because they thought he did not react seriously enough for them. It is strange also to note that for years they talked about my temper tantrum that day. I still cannot understand their thoughts. Temper was the last thing on my mind that day.

CHAPTER 26

LITTLE GIRL SIX YEAR OLD

February 2, 1994

I began my group therapy today. We were told we should keep a daily journal of our thoughts and feelings. I have been doing this all along. We should also record any dreams we have.

A few months ago I began to feel like I was dealing with a little older girl. She seems more mature than my four year old. I was afraid of her. I thought that she would be bad and ugly. I don't know why I felt that way. Perhaps it was because of my memories of being ugly. There was something inside of me that made me believe I needed to be frightened of her.

On a Sunday morning the first part of January, I had a dream. I have decided to record it here as we have been instructed to do so.

I dreamed that I was a single adult, never having married. I lived with my parents. I would lapse into being a little girl every so often. I would hit myself and holler and scream. People would come and look at me. They would pat me on the head. I was the crazy Aunt Norma. "She won't hurt you," my parents said. "She just gets this way sometimes." I was so alone. I literally felt the loneliness in my dream. I had never met Dan.

I woke up and Dan was beside me in bed. I was so relieved. The dream had been so real.

The Little Girl started talking to Dan.

She thanked him for finding Norma. She kept saying, "Don't leave me, don't leave me." She was so frightened of being alone. I don't remember all she talked about that day. Mostly, that she was grateful Dan had found Norma, and of her fear that Dan would leave us. This Little Girl was more mature than my four year old. I believe that she is my six year old.

The following Sunday Little Norma Six Year Old came to visit again. This time she stayed and talked.

She talked a little bit about the Little Little Girl. She said that she had some yucky stuff to talk about, but she didn't want to do it now. She didn't understand how she knew about the Little Little Girl, but she did. This Little Six Year Old Girl had complete faith in her Father in Heaven. She talked of Him like she knew Him. "I'm the one who makes Norma pray to Him," she told Dan. She also said that she was the one who tickled him and made him laugh so hard. She chatted on and on for about 45 minutes. Then she seemed to get tired, but she still wanted to stay. Finally she was gone, almost like a puff of smoke. Gone.

My Little Norma Six Year Old likes to color. One day I was in a department store. We (Little Norma and I) went to the toy department. Nothing seemed familiar. All the toys were so different. Then we saw some Mickey Mouse coloring books. They were familiar. I had a good feeling, a calm feeling, about them. We chose two coloring books and a big box of crayons.

When I told my therapist about the coloring books and crayons, she gave me some coloring books for my Little Girl. She said to color in them whenever I felt comfortable to do so. The books were about childhood sexual abuse. They were to teach children the proper way for touching and that it was okay to say no.

About a week later I took one of the books out and started to color in it. In the picture was a father standing, wearing a suit, a mother in a dress, standing beside the father, holding a baby in her arms. There was a person looking out a window and a little girl standing beside the mother. There were two other children on the sidewalk watching the little girl play hopscotch. A cat was also in the picture.

I began by coloring the suit on the man, then went on to color the woman. I colored very neatly, staying in the lines. Then I colored the baby and finally the little child. I went back to color the father's hair. I colored it neatly and then I started to cry. As I cried, I began to color out the father. Over and over again I colored up and down over the father, from his head to his feet. Then I colored out the mother's ears. Then I scribbled out the person looking out the window. In the picture the Little Girl's hands were lifted up as if reaching for something. I drew in extra arms and hands. The arms had to be down. They could not be up. I changed the smile on her face to a frown. I remember leaving the cat. It was okay to have the cat not destroyed. He did not do anything wrong. The two children watching were scribbled out with black crayon. A few days later I went back to the picture and scribbled out the baby in the woman's arms.

I took this picture to my group therapy session. It may seem strange to say, but I was very proud of my picture. I felt like it was all me. I held nothing back. It felt so good to hold nothing back.

I explained to my group what the picture meant to me. The father was bad. He had to be scribbled out. The mother had to have no ears. She would not hear. The person looking out the window should have helped and did not so she had to be scribbled out. The cat was the only innocent party there. Why did I scribble out the baby? It took me a while to understand that. If it hadn't been for the baby I would not have gone through it. I fought him, until I saw him with her. He couldn't hurt my sisters. If it hadn't been for my sisters, I would have been okay.

I did it to protect my sisters and now they want me to forget it. They want me to pretend that it didn't happen. What a waste of me!

That picture released a lot of emotions for me. I tried some other pictures later but none had the effect on my Little Girl as that one did.

My adult life is feeling pressured. I feel like I cannot handle my life. I want to run away. I often feel this way. I want to be alone, all alone.

CHAPTER 27

SEXUAL FULFILLMENT

February 14, 1994

Today was group therapy again. Right now I am sitting outside Dan's work place waiting for him to join me for lunch. Today in our group session we talked of sex in our life today. This could be a whole book for me.

I have been thinking of this subject all the time I have been driving from therapy to here. I don't want Dan to think that I even think about it. It seems to me that I am really bad if it enters my mind. I feel like less of a person if any sex is involved. I can never initiate it. That would be terrible. That would be dirty. I remember a few months after Dan and I were married, I wondered how long does sex go on. How long before we are too old for this? I was 23 years old. Whenever Dan made love to me, I would close my eyes tight and not be able to open them. Afterwards, I would curl up in a ball in my bed and stay awake for hours. At this time in my life I had no memory of my abuse. My emotions were just crazy.

Having a sexual relationship with my husband is still very difficult for me. I often cry afterwards because it is so emotional for me. If I enjoy it, I feel guilty and dirty. If I don't feel guilty, I often cry because of the lost years I had living in guilt and frustration, not knowing or understanding what was wrong with me.

June 3, 1994

My memories have put a strain on my relationship with Dan. I am very cool towards him. I don't want to be touched and I don't think he wants to touch me. When I go to bed I immediately lay on my side facing away from him. Sometimes we say goodnight. Often we don't. We seem to have an unspoken agreement of not touching each other. We don't talk much. It has been a very trying and long time for Dan. This past New Year's Eve, Dan and the kids went to a party at our friend's and I stayed home. It was the first time in 25 years that Dan and I have not spent New Year's Eve together.

I told Dan that I was worried about our relationship. I am afraid my coolness is driving him away. I can't help it; even though I know the dangers, I continue to be cool.

"It might for a little while, but I will be back because I love you," he told me.

I know he feels it. I think he just doesn't have the energy to handle my problems anymore. I feel so alone, so alone.

CHAPTER 28

ANGER

March 9, 1994

When Dan came home from work today I was angry with him. I wanted him with me when I needed him, but he wasn't there. I knew there was no logical reason for my anger, yet it was there.

I want a teddy bear. I'm angry because I don't have one.

I told Dan today that I don't want to be married. I don't want to have kids. I don't want to take care of anyone. I just want someone to take care of me.

Oh, please someone take care of me. Don't let him do it to me anymore.

This is such a confusing time for me as well as for Dan. It is as though the Little Norma and the Adult Norma are both feeling the same emotions. One is feeling them in an adult way and the other in a childish way. I am feeling both the childish anger and the adult anger at the same time. It is very, very frustrating.

I want a teddy bear. I must have one. I look for just the right one every time I go into a store. Sometimes I go shopping just to find my teddy bear.

I found my teddy bear, a dark brown bear with happy eyes and a red bow around his neck. He has great big paws that I love. I call him Bear.

CHAPTER 29

LETTERS

March 10, 1994

Two weeks ago we were assigned in our group therapy session to write letters to the perpetrators. I have put this off as long as I can. I have been frightened to do this assignment. I have been worried that it would set me back in my healing. In my journal I wrote the date and time I began my letter to my father. These letters may seem fragmented to others reading them now, but they were my thoughts, feelings and emotions at the time they were written.

March 10, 1994 — 10:43 am

Dad,

Why did you do those things to me? Did you think it made me happy? Did you think it made me someone I wasn't?

I did not like it. I did it only to protect Penny and Bonnie. I did not want to happen to them what happened to me.

I hate you daddy. Because of you I have no mother now. I would love to have a relationship with a mother.

She could not or would not protect me over you. I hate her for that.

Penny has taken your side. I don't even know if she wants to talk to me again. I have always been close to Bonnie. Now I don't even talk to her because my healing is so much a part of my life, and she cannot handle to talk about it.

So, dad, even as I am an adult, you are still taking from me. How selfish can anyone be?

Where is my childhood? I had none. You took that from me. I was a sad little girl and you didn't even know it.

You said, "That feels good, doesn't it, Norma?" Did you really think that you were doing that for me? Now you tell me you don't remember it at all? How can I hate you when you don't even understand what my hate is about?

When Stephanie was two weeks old, we moved from our home in Port Huron. The Lord said, "Move," and we listened and moved. For 20 years I wondered why. Now I know. You were the reason. The Lord would not let you do to my children what you did to me.

When mom says she is so sad because she never had her grandchildren near her, making me feel guilty for moving away, it was your fault, not mine. Just like all those times you were with me. It was your fault. Not mine.

(Here I wrote to my mother, I couldn't help it, it just came out.)

Oh, mama, it was not my fault. Can't you see that? It was never my fault.

(I cried here before I could continue writing.)

Please, mama, I wanted a hug, not to be slapped. Please protect me, not him. Oh, mama, it wasn't my fault, it wasn't my fault.

There were times, daddy, did you know, that I wanted to kill you? I thought of different ways to do it. But I never could.

Did you know, daddy, that I did try to kill myself? That was easier than trying to kill you.

You have taken away my family. You have taken away my childhood. You stole my innocence in the name of love. You made my adult life so difficult.

But I will have the last say. I will be healed. Not for anything that you have done to help. You couldn't do that, my "innocent" father.

But because of me.

I shall be the victor!

Finally!

Norma

11:08 am

I wrote this letter in 25 minutes. I started to write and did not stop until I was finished.

After I wrote my letter I reread it about three times. Each time I reread it, I felt better. I kept emptying myself.

I thought writing the letter would ruin my day. It didn't. I felt better than I had felt in a long time. I felt energy even. Will I give it to him? I don't know. I can wait on that.

March 31, 1994

I decided to write to my sister Bonnie.

March 31, 1994 — 3:15 pm

My big sister,

I could never say no to you. When we lived together in California, it was always what you wanted. I wanted to live in Anaheim and work at Disneyland. I don't even think I mentioned it to you because you had a job in Los Angeles.

You were always so strong inside. You were stronger inside than you were weak outside. I think you knew that also.

We were always so close after we grew up. I don't remember if we were close as children growing up. I just don't remember my childhood. I don't remember doing anything together. I remember our neighbor, Sandra. I remember you two playing jacks and I couldn't play with you. I don't remember why it hurt so much, but it really did.

I really enjoyed working with you in San Marino. I believe it brought out the best in me. I became self assured and felt in control of myself and my circumstances. I want to thank you for that opportunity.

I enjoyed our trips to Santa Barbara and staying at the Holiday Inn on the ocean. I felt like somebody. I guess I am even thankful for Martha and Marilyn because I had a dream with them. I have learned that I can live with failure, but I cannot live without hope.

I am sorry that our relationship seems to be dwindling away. I'm sure you think it is my need for solitude, to be away from all my past.

That is not the reason. The reason I have to stay away is because I cannot deal with your not dealing. When my first memories came back in Marietta, I felt the love and support of you and George and Penny. But, later, I guess, it just got too difficult for all of you.

When I came back to visit you, I needed a big sister to understand and to listen. You didn't want to listen. You didn't say that, but it showed and I felt it. You listened a little, but I felt the distance between us as we talked. I really wanted and thought I needed you to really hear what I was saying. But I didn't need it, because I am surviving without it.

I guess the greatest hurt of all was when you refused to read my journal. I still cry over that. That was me I was giving to you. Only Dan and I had read it. And you. I wanted to share it with you. I am really sorry you didn't have the strength to deal with it.

You all think I need to forgive and get on with my life. Do you know, Bonnie, when I was little all I went through to protect you? The Little Girl never expected anything in return. I don't think she ever thought about you knowing what she did for you. The older girl, me—now—did expect some comfort—at least acknowledging it enough to discuss it without distance in thought and words.

Perhaps you may not understand what I am saying. But I think if you search your soul you will know. You will know I needed you, and you could not or would not allow yourself to become emotionally involved with me.

I have truly had more emotional support from friends I have known for a short time than from my family. That makes me bitter. That makes me angry, but most of all that makes me sad.

I guess I am jealous. Jealous of the closeness the rest of the family have felt toward each other caused by this remembering. You have all strengthened each other through this. But me, I'm on the outside.

Penny says that it is my choice. I guess it is. It is my choice to stay away rather than act like it never happened.

I guess I can feel like the Little Girl accomplished what she sat out to do. She did indeed save you from the abuse enough to protect you in your adult life.

I am grateful for that. I truly am. I'm just so sad that she protected you so much that you are not strong enough emotionally to deal with her now. I don't know if that hurt will ever go away. If it does, perhaps we can be sisters and friends again. If it doesn't, I don't know.

I know that I must deal with my own life and writing this letter was important for me to do. I am very disappointed and hurt, Bonnie, and you don't even know or comprehend. Perhaps I will always be the black sheep now. We will have to wait and see.

Your sister, Norma

It took me thirty minutes to write this letter. A lot of emotions came out of me in those thirty minutes.

I decided to write a letter to my mother also. I talked to my Little Girl and told her to say whatever she felt like saying to my mother. This is her letter to her mama. All those times her mama wouldn't listen, she can tell her now.

March 31, 1994 — 4:00 pm

Dear Mama,

How could you protect him and blame me. I was so little. How could you think those things about me?

Do you know, mama, what you thought and said hurt me more than what he did to me. He was gentle with me. He talked softly to me. He treated me in a way that made me feel good, but bad too. Mama, do you know how confusing that is?

Mama, I wanted to be hugged like a little girl. Daddy couldn't do that. Mama, I wanted to be a little girl. I wanted to be a good little girl.

Mama, you told me to take care of Bonnie. She was weak. She was not strong. I had to take care of her.

He came to me, mama, in the big house in Croswell. I was really little. Aunt Norma was upstairs. I didn't like what he was doing to me. I made a lot of noise. I kicked him. I hit him. He told me, mama, to shut up or Aunt Norma would hear. I didn't shut up. I hollered louder, maybe Aunt Norma would hear. He slapped my face and left the room.

Then I heard Bonnie cry. Mama, he was on top of Bonnie. He made her cry. She didn't cry loud like me.

I couldn't let him do that to her anymore. I decided, mama, to protect her like you told me to.

She was my sister, mama. I couldn't let him hurt her again. I knew that it was my fault that he had hurt Bonnie. It was my fault that she was crying. I couldn't let him do it to her again. If he did it to me, he wouldn't do it to her.

Do you know, mama, that that hurts a little girl? Where were you?

Penny was little. I remember when I saw him with her. I cried, "Oh, no, not Penny to." I had so many things to watch for. How could I watch them all? I had to go to him so he would not go to them, because I could not watch them both all the time.

I was so confused. You finally saw us. We were in the little bedroom. He was lying on the floor. I was kneeling beside him with his thing in my hand. I was moving it up and down. He wanted me to put it in my mouth. You came in just before I did that. Mama, I was so happy to see you. I must have looked happy. You would protect me now.

Mama, you sent me to my room. You bawled him out. Then, mama, you came in to me. You were going to hug me. I sat up from lying on the bed. You slapped me, mama. I scrambled to the far side of the bed. "No, mama, no."

You were so mad at me. I didn't understand why you were so mad at me. You told me to take care of Bonnie. Penny was the baby. I had to take care of her to. But, mama, why were you mad at me?

I wanted to die. No matter what daddy did to me it couldn't be worse than what you did to me that day. You blamed me!! You said I was a bad girl. You were mad at me!

I was not a bad girl, mama. I tried so hard to be good. I tried so hard to protect my sisters. Why didn't he do those things to you instead of me?

He talked about you, mama. Did you know that? He didn't really want me. He wanted you.

I should have blamed you instead of you blaming me. Mama, I was a better person than you were. I didn't blame you, but you blamed me.

I hate you for all those things. I hate you for your clean house and the times you spent cleaning it. I hate you for not knowing I wanted a teddy bear. I hate you for loving him more than me because he was bad and I was good. I hate you for not taking care of me.

I'm sorry I was never good enough for you. Maybe, mama, you are starting to make yourself happy. I couldn't try to do that anymore.

I said the day I tried to kill myself, "Good bye, mama." I say it again, but this time because I want to live.

Good bye mama.

Norma

I never mailed any of these letters.

CHAPTER 30

LOSSES

April 27, 1994

I feel a need to cry tonight. I have wanted to all day long. When I arrived home at 6:00 this evening everything was hectic. It continued to get worse through the night. I want to cry. I need space.

I had a dream this morning that I was going crazy. It was so real. I always have that fear deep inside of me.

I am never alone. Wendy needs a strong mother now and I am not giving her what she needs. I am not giving anyone what they need. All I can think of is that I need to be alone.

Bonnie called me this morning to tell me that her son, David, is getting married. It was very difficult for me to talk with her. When I heard her voice I thought, "Oh, no, why did I answer the phone." There is always a strain between us.

I have no extended family. I don't see any cousins or aunts and uncles anymore. I just can't do it for some reason. I saw an aunt and uncle in the grocery store a few months ago. It upset me so much I could not finish my shopping. I left everything in the store and went home and cried.

I am afraid that the longer I put off seeing my parents and my sisters the harder it will be to see them. Still, I know that I cannot deal with seeing or speaking to them now. My children want to know if we are going to David's wedding. I don't know if I can handle it. They want to go.

I feel inside of me another crisis coming up. I get that feeling every so often. I feel it strongly now.

April 29, 1994

Another Mother's Day is coming around. How will I do this year? Last year we went away. What will we do this year? I feel like I have to hide on Mother's Day. I have always been depressed on Mother's Day. I never could understand that. Even when my children were small, I felt like crying on Mother's Day.

About two weeks ago I went into denial again. I told Dan that none of this stuff happened to me. It could not. I went on for about ten minutes telling him how impossible it all is.

I can't believe my mother and my Little Girl. They don't agree. I can't believe them both. There must not be a Little Girl. I have to believe my mother.

At this point I started to sob. I cried uncontrollably. I've hurt my Little Girl. I've hurt my Little Girl. Nobody believes her. Not even me. I'm going crazy. I screamed this loudly. I'm going crazy! I sat on the floor screaming, holding my hands over my ears while shaking my head back and forth. I'm going crazy! I'm going crazy!

Finally Dan said, "You are not going crazy, Norma. It happened."

I began to calm down. I felt guilty for putting my Little Girl through denial again.

Later the thought came to me. The choice is not to believe my Little Girl or my mother. The choice is to believe me or my mother. The Little Girl is me. Why is this so difficult for me to comprehend?

I wonder if I will ever see my parents again. I wonder sometimes how they are. Are they sick? Are they okay? The few times I talk to my sisters, they never mention them. My children never mention them. I miss them. I have truly lost so much. I feel like I have lost my entire extended family in the past year. My life will never be the same. I must acknowledge that fact. It can never be the same again between my parents, my sisters, and me. It doesn't matter how much I want it to be, it just is not possible.

CHAPTER 31

IT HURTS! IT HURTS!

May 1994

My Little Girl is changing. I feel differently when she is with me than I felt when the four-year-old Little Girl was with me. She is more mature, more contemplative, not so young. I spoke with my Older Little Girl and told her that I wanted her to talk to me. I want her to tell me what she is thinking about. I am anxious to get to know her.

Little Norma is speaking here.

I hate the summer. I miss Mrs. Lewis. (Mrs. Lewis was my first grade teacher.) *She was so nice and kind to me. I really loved her. Now I am at home all the time. I am afraid at home. He's here a lot, but he works a lot to so I don't have to worry then. It is not as bad as I thought it was going to be. She is here all the time to. That makes me feel safe. He won't let her catch him with me again. He is afraid of her. I can be thankful for that.*

I don't like her. She makes me feel uncomfortable, but when she is around, he doesn't touch me. I hate him.

I want to have fun. I want to play. I want her to be around, but not near me.

When mama goes away he comes to me. I'm not scared like I was when I was real little. If I just try not to feel it maybe I won't.

That doesn't work. I do feel it. It hurts. It hurts so much. Can't he see how much it hurts me? I can't tell mama though. She would think that I was a bad girl again. I'm not a bad girl. I am not a bad girl!

I was sitting on the floor, crying. My Little six-year-old Girl likes to sit on the floor. Most of the time when she comes to me, I slide on the floor and sit while she talks.

As I was talking about how he hurt me, I started to cry. Soon I was screaming. I cried and screamed, "No! No! Stay away from me!" I pushed myself back towards the wall. "I'll tell mommy if you don't stay away from me."

After this memory I cried and cried. It was not the frantic sobbing of my Little Girl Four Year Old. It was the heartbreaking cry of a six year old. After a while, my Little Girl Six Year Old left, and I got up from the floor and sat on the chair. I cried and cried.

My Little Girl Six Year Old came back. I slid back to the floor while crying. Soon I was on my stomach sobbing. Then the crying stopped. I felt light after this episode.

During the past few months I have had times of crying over pain. I don't feel the pain. I feel the emotion of the pain. I say over and over again. "It hurts! It hurts! It hurts!"

I have always tried very hard to not have my children see me when I am having memories. But one day I started to cry and Wendy was with me. I cried and cried on her shoulder. "It hurts so bad, it hurts so bad." I repeated this over and over again as I cried with Wendy comforting me.

I believe that by the time the Little Girl was six years old she had been penetrated a number of times by her father. It never stopped hurting. The Little Girl thought it should stop hurting, but it never did. He hurt her every time he went inside of her.

How could I feel sorry for him now? That is what he wants. "I have never been so hurt in my life," he said to me about my memories. How can I feel sorry for him? The dirty son of a bitch, the bastard, to hurt a Little Girl like that for his own gratification. I think it is time for me to be enraged at him for what he did. He wants me to feel sorry for him, for his hurting. Poor daddy, poor daddy. Poor daddy, for what? He doesn't cry in remorse. He cries for himself, not for me.

(As I later read this part of my journal, I remember writing those words. I don't speak that way, but I think it was an older girl I felt here. I have a Fourteen Year Old who used words like that.)

CHAPTER 32

FREE

July 9, 1994

I spent some time at the lake today. I love going there. I can think and relax and rest my soul. On the way home I began to think about my Little Girl and her thoughts about her mother. Did she really try to tell her mama? Was she too frightened? I decided to ask her.

I pulled the car over to a parking spot along the lake. Then I took out my journal and wrote to the Little Girl.

Little Girl, I want you to tell me when and how you told your mama. I will believe you. I will understand your hurt. Please tell me and I will write it down.

I was scared. I tried to tell her. We lived in Croswell. Right after daddy hurt Bonnie, I told mama that daddy had hurt Bonnie when mama was away. She said, "Daddy wouldn't hurt Bonnie!" I said he did. She told me to be nice and not to be jealous. Daddy loved us all.

I tried to tell her again in the house across the street from the lighthouse. I saw him with Penny. I told mama that daddy was doing something bad to Penny. She told me to stop saying things like that. Daddy was a good daddy. He loved us all. I shouldn't be jealous of the time he spent with my sisters.

She was a stupid woman. She thought I was jealous of the time he spent with them.

The adult Norma became very emotional as I wrote the following lines.

I had to stop it. I had to stop it. He kept hurting them. I wouldn't let him hurt them anymore. Mama won't stop him. I couldn't stop him. The only thing I could do was to kill him. Then he would stop.

We had a big knife in the kitchen. I would hold it in my hand. I wanted to take it to bed with me but I was afraid I would be the one to die. So I never took it to bed with me.

I was not a bad girl! I was not a bad girl! Even if I killed him I would not be a bad girl. He did bad things to my sisters and me, and nobody would stop him. I couldn't. I was too afraid.

The Little Girl was so ashamed of herself for being too frightened to kill her father.

Sunday July 10, 1994

I could not go to church today. I was still too upset over my past memories and emotions. The adult Norma felt guilty for having murder in her heart.

I sat in the living room and reread my memories of the Little Girl telling her mother. I became very distressed. I felt panic. I became frightened that I would go over the edge and not come back. I called Dan at church and, sobbing, asked him to come home. I went back to the living room and sat down in a chair. I was almost in a trance. I stared out the front window, watching the driveway and waited for Dan to get home. It took him about ten minutes to drive from church to home. All the time I was waiting I stared out the window. I kept saying over and over until he arrived, "He hurt me so bad I want him to die. He hurt me so bad I want him to die."

When I saw Dan pull into the driveway I said, "Danny will protect me. I don't need to kill him. Danny will protect me I don't need to kill him."

Dan rushed into the house and knelt down in front of me. I sobbed in his arms and said, "You'll protect me Danny. Won't you? You won't let him hurt me!" I cried and cried, "You'll protect me Danny. Won't you? You won't let him hurt me." I cried so hard it was difficult to breathe. I rubbed his back as he was on his knees in front of me. I looked him in the eyes and begged him to protect me. Then I rested my head on his shoulder before the whole cycle began again. I cried and cried. Not the sobbing of my Little Girl Four Year Old, but the sad sobbing of my Little Girl Six Year Old.

Finally the crying was over. I felt lighter and freer than I had in months. That afternoon Dan and I went for a ride and visited my Grandmother. It was the first time I had been able to visit any of my relatives in months. We took her for a drive and bought her an ice cream cone.

When we arrived home the kids were there. We played air hockey. I laughed and laughed. It felt so good to laugh.

I was able to be in control as an adult. I felt self assurance that I can never remember feeling before. Dan and I had a disagreement about a few things that night. It was the first time in my life I ever felt secure enough to disagree with anyone. I felt light. I felt free.

Thank you Little Girl for freeing me the way that you have. I don't know if there is much more for my Little Girl Six Year Old to tell me. I do know that I have an older one waiting to talk to me.

CHAPTER 33

ANGER AGAIN

July 12, 1994

I want to run away for good, never to come back. I can't handle it any more. I have been a failure all my life.

I couldn't keep him from them. I couldn't keep him from me. I couldn't kill him. I couldn't tell my mama what I thought. I can't heal right. I can't do anything right. I can't clean house. I can't do laundry. I can't cook. I can't buy groceries.

I hate you, dad, for what you have done to me. I hate you for taking away my childhood. I want to be a child now. How can I? I have five kids, one husband and no money. I can't afford to do anything fun. I could never even say what I feel because of you. You stunted me, you dirty bastard. I still have a Little Girl inside of me who wants to be taken care of. All she ever did was to care for somebody else. Watch you. Watch her sisters. Watch her mama. She couldn't see you with me again. What would happen to me then? You dirty old man! I wanted to be a little girl. I wanted to laugh. Not to worry. You deserved to die then, but I was too afraid. I failed there too. I knew that you were too big and I was too little. You dirty old man.

Why didn't I die when I was little? What have I got? I have an old car, a house I can't afford to finish, a dead garden, a broken lawnmower, and a boat that doesn't work. I have a husband who loves me and who has to work all of the time. I drag him down. He can't even make love to me without me crying.

I have to run away. I can't stand it anymore. But, I can't be gone forever and when I come back, it's just as I left it. All bad!

July 27, 1994

Red is my angry color. That is the color I used for writing in my journal today.

Why am I so angry? We are getting ready to go camping. Everyone is excited. Even Scott is spending more time at home and seems to enjoy it.

I am scared about camping. I am scared about getting ready. Why am I so frightened of everything? I don't want to go!

I'm angry! Why am I angry?

I want someone to comfort me. They understand, but they don't comfort me. That is what I wanted from Bonnie when I visited her last year. She couldn't give that to me. I wanted my mother and father to comfort me when I went to tell them I wanted to die. They couldn't do it. I comfort my children when they have problems. I WANT TO BE COMFORTED!

Dan tries. He listens, he holds me. But something is missing. My Little Girl needs to be comforted as a Little Girl, not as an adult.

I need to get away. I need to be alone. I don't want anyone near me ever. Maybe when the children are gone, I will divorce Dan. He is wonderful to me, but I need to be alone, all alone.

July 28, 1994

Daddy hurts me. He hurts me. I didn't want to hurt. I didn't want him doing those things to me. He put his thing inside of me. It felt like something too big was there. It hurt. I was too little for it. Why didn't he know it was too big for me? If I put it in my mouth I wanted to throw up. If he put it inside of me, it hurt. Both were bad. But he said I liked it. Did I like it? It hurt. But he was gentle with me, but it hurt! Please leave me alone daddy. Please don't do this anymore. I want to sleep and not be tired. I want to laugh and have fun and not feel dirty and bad. Little girls aren't supposed to be bad. Little Girls are supposed to laugh and giggle and have friends. Where are my friends? I don't have time for friends. I'm afraid to have friends come over. What if they find out I am bad? Then they won't be my friends anymore. Oh, daddy, I want to die. Do you know that? You make me want to die.

As I wrote these last few pages, my head was on my arm, my arm on the table. Then I dropped the pen and rested my head on my book and cried.

August 19, 1994

I was sitting on my chair in my bedroom today. I began to rock. I cried and cried and continued to rock. Stacy came in to me. I told her I was all right. She left to get her father.

Dan came in. By this time I was sitting on the floor sobbing loudly. He had been working on Stephanie's car and his cloths were oily. He knows that the smell of oil brings back bad memories. He shut the bedroom door and took off his clothes, washed his hands and face, and came to me in his underwear. He sat on the floor beside me.

Please don't hurt me again! Please don't hurt me again. I don't have to love him. Mama said I have to love my daddy. I don't have to love him!

I'm in the fourth grade. Miss Randall is my teacher. I don't like her. But I think I really do. She comes to our house for dinner one night. She brings really good fudge. I want to tell her about daddy, but I'm afraid. I'm afraid she will think I'm a bad girl. I don't want her to think that. Frank is in my class. He gave me a piggy bank for my birthday with a penny in it. He is my friend. I don't want anyone to think I'm a bad girl. I sit in the middle of the classroom. The windows look out over the grass in the front of the classroom. I think it is the second or third classroom from the front door.

I feel like the innocent little girl is gone. I don't feel innocent anymore. I am very angry. I don't worry about Bonnie anymore. He doesn't bother her. Her handicap shows more now. He doesn't like that. I'm grateful I don't have to worry about her anymore. I am still confused. I hate him. I hate him. I know now that I can never kill him. Nobody will ever listen to me. I have no choice in my life. I want to die. I can't do that. I am too afraid. I just have to do whatever he says. There is nobody to help me. I feel so isolated, so sad, so depressed. I can never be happy.

As I would read and reread these last few lines and paragraphs, I kept thinking that isolated and depressed were pretty big words for my six year old to be using. As I reread it again, I realized that this Little Girl is not six years old. She is in the fourth grade. When did she grow up? How long have I been dealing with this older child? I think she began talking to me on August 19th. Now I must get to know my Little Ten Year Old better, another new challenge for me.

Little Norma Ten Year Old, thank you for talking with me and letting me get to know you. I love you.

CHAPTER 34

TO STAY MARRIED OR NOT

September 1, 1994

My life with Dan is better. Our vacation was a nightmare. It was so bad it was funny. Even before we left, almost everything broke down. By the time we made it to the camp ground, what hadn't broken down at home and was fixed, broke down there. We finally left the park a day early in the rain, and we were all grateful to be home.

We gave the kids money to go to Taco Bell and the movies. We went for a ride and had a Dairy Queen. Dan and I had a good talk as we were sitting by the river eating our ice cream. I was able to be completely honest with him. I told him I didn't know if I wanted to work on our marriage. I didn't know if it was worth trying to save. He said he believed it was. He wanted to stay married.

This may sound strange here. I am so selfish. Dan has worked so hard with me. He has never once lost his temper with me in the two years I have been working through my trials. In fact he has never once lost his temper with me in all the 26 years we have been married. So why am I talking about divorce. I really don't know.

He told me that he loved me very much and that our marriage was very important to him. I told him I would have to think about it.

A few days later I told him that I wanted to work on our marriage and try to save it.

We shared or thoughts on making love. He said he would never push me. "You have had enough of that," were his words. He even puts off touching me. I felt he didn't care anymore. He was trying to protect me from further hurt. One night last week I reached over and kissed him. We made love. It was calm and peaceful and nice.

CHAPTER 35

SEX

October 10, 1994

Today I finished Christmas shopping for Jared. We have to mail it out this week to get to Korea by Christmas. After shopping I went down to the river to sit for a while. I have been reading *Survivors and Partners*. It has been very helpful. Dan and I still have very little, almost no, sex life. I have put off this part of my healing. It frightens me. I must analyze my thinking about sex.

To me it is dirty. Sex should not be enjoyed. If I enjoy it I am bad. It is very bad to do it with someone you love. It makes that love dirty. I feel insecure, embarrassed, guilty, and dirty about sexual expression. I have never enjoyed sex, but since my memories have begun to return I am more self conscience about it. When Dan touches me I pull away or pretend I am asleep. He always respects my boundaries. It must be very difficult for him.

In my memories I always felt like I hated my father. There must have been some love there also. I loved him. I wanted him to be my daddy. I loved him and he had sex with me. I hated the act. Love and sex cannot go together. If you have sex it would be better to have it with someone who is a stranger to you.

What a perverse way of thinking! I believe that love comes first, then marriage, then sex. I believe that. Why do I feel like love and sex cannot go together? I know in my head that is wrong. I know that my abuse has made me feel this way. I know in my head that I love Dan and that sex with the man I love is right. Will I ever be able to feel inside of me, in my very soul, that love and sex are both gifts from God and that they go together? I hope so.

CHAPTER 36

ON WITH MY LIFE

October 11, 1994

Last night I came home from shopping and told Dan that I believed I have reached my deepest, darkest memories and emotions, and I am on my way up now. I am on the side of the hill heading up. There will be valleys, I know, but I believe the worst is over. It has taken me almost two years to come to this point.

My mother and sisters had said they believed me, and then they later changed their minds. When they believed me, it was such an emotional lift to my spirit. Months later when Bonnie told me that she believed my memories were in my head and from reading books and watching television shows about abuse, the intense hurt returned.

I almost went back into denial. She is my older sister. She is so wise and smart. She must be right, and I am making this up. I cried and cried that day. My parents and sisters talk to each other. They don't talk to me. I am sure they all feel the same way.

I felt like a bad little girl being chastised for doing something wrong when Bonnie was talking to me. She said that I was not only hurting myself and my children with my memories, but also hurting them. She said she believed it seemed real to me, but that it could not be real. Nothing like that could have happened in our home. She reminded me of the news articles of women having repressed memories and years later retracting it all saying it was a mistake. She said their therapists had put it all in their minds.

I had told them over and over again that my memories began before I ever saw a therapist. In fact, Bonnie, Penny and George were all with me when my first memories came to me. They all seemed to forget that Penny was the first one to have memories.

The greatest hurt that day came when she told me that if she were me she would not have allowed all that hurt in her life. She would have found medication or something, but she would not have put herself or her family through the trauma I was putting them all through.

To the adult Norma and the Little Girl it was her fault all over again, her fault for the hurt. No matter how hard she tried she could not stop the pain. It is still her fault.

I wrote the following letter to Bonnie the next day. I never mailed it, but I felt so much better after writing it.

October 12, 1994

Dear Bonnie,

Thank you for calling me back yesterday. I think that we needed that talk. In some ways I am pleased that you called, and in other ways I am sorry.

I have thought a lot about the things you said. I don't really think I made you understand any of my feelings, but I believe I understand many of yours.

I said that I had spent about a year feeling like you feel. That is about it being real. It never entered my mind that what I was reading was causing my memories. My reading was like my therapy. It helped me to understand what I was already going through. That is in the past tense. I had suffered these feelings before I read about them. The majority of my memories were before most of my reading.

How could it have happened? I have asked myself that question thousands of times. I am sure that all people living through repressed memories ask themselves that question. It was hard for me to accept. Bonnie, it is not easy to accept. Thankfully, you will never have to. Don't try to. I do, though, because it is me that it is happening to. So my feelings are just a little bit more involved here.

You spoke about the book, *Reach for the Rainbow*, and how so many of the things that I say are happening to me are like the things that she wrote about in this book. I only had the book a short time before I came to visit you and had only read a small part of it. What I did read seemed to reach me in a way I did not understand. I thought it would help you and Penny. That is why I bought a copy for both of you. As I read it with Dan, later, after some of my memories and emotions came back, we would say, "Yeah ." I was not getting ideas from the book. I was getting understanding about what I had already experienced.

You mentioned the movie about the sisters being protected. I never saw it or even heard of it until you told me about it.

Do you see what I am doing? I am justifying my pain to you. Like I have to explain to you why I hurt to be sure that you understand that it is real to me. What a bunch of crap. I don't need to justify my pain to you or to anyone.

What about our dreams, the cold water? What about Penny saying when Bob touched her breasts, "No daddy, don't do that." What about the hotdog you remember was under the blanket in your bed?" Have you forgotten that? What about his tongue in Penny's mouth?

I don't want to persuade you that our father molested me, or you, for that matter. I don't need to do that. To be honest, I don't really give a damn about how you feel right now about all of this.

When I hung up the phone after talking to you, it was the same thing all over again. Not the exact words that you said, but the meaning was the same to me. It is my fault that you are hurting over this. "If it were me, I would have found a way so I would not have to deal with the pain." The pain I was causing for me and my family and for you and my extended family as well. It is my fault. That is what you said to me before I hung up.

Take a pill. What kind of pill, Bonnie? What kind of a pill do you take to stop having memories? Did I ever think of asking you to take a pill to make you stronger? I accepted you and loved you with your physical handicap and never thought of blaming you for the pain you felt yourself or caused the rest of our family to feel because of your handicap. We all hurt emotionally because you were not strong enough to do the things we could do. Often we did not do things because you could not do them. I could not stop my emotional pain with a pill anymore than you could stop your handicap with a pill.

The one question I asked in both my group therapy and my individual therapy is how can it be real? I must be imagining it. Their answer was, "Norma, can you imagine the emotional trauma you experienced with the memory? Could you have made that up?" I say to you, Bonnie, what I said to them, "No." There is no way I could make up that emotion.

I am sure that you all agree that somehow in my reading and watching movies that my mind has conjured up my pain. "Yes, my pain is real to me, but not caused by real pain." That is what you said to me, Bonnie. I must admit when you said that to me, it surprised and hurt me very much. I have suspected that is how you felt, but never would admit it to myself.

I wish I could join you in your dreamland. If what I am saying hurts you, I am sorry, Bonnie. I truly am sorry. It is not now, nor ever has been my desire to hurt anyone. But I cannot pretend any longer. So if you think that means that I must heal no matter how much I hurt others. So be it. You could not and would not read my journal until you were ready. That hurt me for months. My pain could not compel you to read my journal, so I guess I could say the same about you. Your welfare came before mine, no matter how much I hurt. I am only saying that so perhaps you will understand my meaning when I said, "I have to heal to matter how much it may make someone else hurt." No matter what I said to you, Bonnie, you would not read my journal because you were not strong enough. I can say, even though it hurt me, it was right for you, so that makes it right for me. I guess that is all I am asking of you. I am writing a book from my journal. I am sorry I cannot send you a copy of my first draft, but I know if you read it you will say the same things you said about my journal. It hurts me too much to hear you say those things. See you hurt me too, Bonnie. Pain is a part of my life. It is a part of all of our lives. But pain can make us stronger.

I cannot go back. I have hurt too much. I have worked too hard for the last two years to be in vain. I will go on. I will be better. I will continue my marriage and I will be happy.

I survived incest! I can conquer anything.

I love you, Bonnie.

Love,

Your sister, Norma

CHAPTER 37

REACHING FOR MY RAINBOW

October 11, 1994

Lynne Finney said in *Reach for the Rainbow* that a memory would come back that would be so real that you could never deny your memories again. It was not a memory exactly for me, but an understanding of the situation, and a calmness that I felt when this understanding finally came to me.

I believe, now, that my mother never saw my father penetrate me. She was very angry with what she did see, but I don't believe that she felt it hurt me. I think that she wanted to believe it would never happen again and so to her understanding it did not happen again.

Many of the memories the Little Girl had of that day her mama came in and saw the Little Girl with her father were her frightened thoughts. Her mama didn't want her to drown! Yet the frightened child believed this to be the fact.

Because her mama didn't hold her and reassure her that it would never happen again and because her mama made her feel that she was responsible for the abuse by calling her a bad girl and making her promise to never to that again, the Little Girl was so confused and so emotionally hurt that she truly believed there was nothing left in this life for her.

She was frightened of the threats her father had made to her. There was always the dream of the cold dark water. The day she began to fear the water and could no longer play in the water without thinking she was going to drown. Of course her father would not drown her, but in her young mind she believed what she had been told by her father that if anyone found out... And so, the Little Girl felt there was nothing else to do. She would drown herself in the warm bathtub.

After that day, the Little Girl's life changed. She knew she could never depend on her mother to help her. There had always been, previously, that secret hope. She also knew that now she not only had to watch her two sisters to keep her father away from them, but she also had to be sure that her mama never found her with her father again.

In many ways the Little Girl grew up that day. She was no longer a Little Girl yearning to be an innocent small child, she was now a Little Girl with grown-up responsibilities and no hope for help.

The most difficult part of the Little Girl's life was not the sexual molestation of her father. It was her youthful belief that her mama thought she was bad. "*She is not a bad girl*," she has cried hundreds of times. She could handle what her daddy did, but not what her mama thought.

It was also the unending, frustrating feeling of the need to protect her sisters, and her continual belief that she failed to do this.

I know that my parents were not evil people. One of the hardest things for me to try to comprehend while recovering my memories was the idea of my parents being evil. The parents I grew up with were not bad people. Yet in my head and in my heart I believed that child molesters had to be evil. How could I work this balance out in my mind?   This question was one of my main causes for continual relapses into denial.

My parents were not evil. They loved me as they loved my sisters. My father worked hard to support our family. My mother worked hard and did the best she could to make our home happy. They did the best they could with what they had available to them.

Any person you see on the street may be a child molester. They can do many good things in their lives and still molest children. That does not excuse them for what they do.

I am not excusing my father for what he did to me. The act was evil. It damaged me for the rest of my life. One thing in healing that I yearned for, and have never received, was an apology from my father for that harm. But an apology would mean admittance and that was not possible for him. I forgive them for the pain I felt throughout my childhood and adult life. This forgiveness does them no good until they can admit to the abuse of the Little Girl. In fact, this forgiveness made them angry. The forgiveness is for me and for my growth. I can now take a step further in my process of healing.

One of the most important things I have learned in these past two years is that we must hate the act of child molestation, but we do not need to hate the molester. Almost every child molester was molested as a child. How sad it is. Child molestation will continue to plague our society until we can heal the molester.

The threads of my memory are finally beginning to weave a clear picture for me. There are still many memories that I do not have. I do not remember a childhood. Perhaps I never will.

I can now begin to feel differently towards my mother. She had no idea of my terror that day when she came into my bedroom. A Little Girl was waiting to be comforted, protected, and hugged. She received none of these things. The Little Girl could not forgive her mother for denying her this love.

My father was molested as a child. He needed help to overcome the damage that was done to him. He did not receive it.

I understand my parents much better now. More importantly, I understand my Little Girls.

I love my parents. I love my Little Girls. I love me.

CHAPTER 38

WILL IT REALLY EVER BE OVER?

September 18, 2009

I had my book in a box for a number of years. As I retyped it and revised it, it brought back many memories. I am very happy now. I am whole. My Little Girls are a part of me. In fact I feel pretty lucky. Many people forget the little ones they used to be. My Little Girls are still very real to me. Dan and I bought an old house last year that was built in 1880. We are restoring it. One bedroom upstairs is going to be a Little Girl's room. When I began planning it, I was not consciously thinking of my Little Girls, but as I began working again on my book, I realized who the bedroom was for. Dan and I were shopping a few weeks ago. I found an old doll carriage. I had to have it. On our way home I said, "You know who had to have that!" His reply was, "Yes, I do."

I think to complete this book I need to share a few more episodes in my life.

January 21, 1998

I had two very unusual dreams. I think they began my journey again to myselves.

January 25, 1998

Today is my day. I skipped church and went to a show of toy farm equipment. I enjoyed it. Now I'm at the St. Clair River near the Blue Water Bridge. I think I'll take a walk and then decide what to do.

Well I have taken my walk and driven to my beach. I'm not sure what to do now. I guess I'm a little afraid. I haven't talked with Little Norma for a long time. I don't even know if she will talk to me.

Little Norma decided she would talk to me:

I know my daddy is dying. I see my mama with him. It serves her right to have to take care of him now. It was always him and not me. I'm not sad that he is dying. I wanted him to die a long time ago. I couldn't do it. He won't hurt anybody ever again. I am glad of that.

I think of Grandpa. I was glad when he died. I knew I shouldn't be, but I didn't have to worry about him any more then. He was good to me but I was afraid of him, afraid of the room upstairs. He never hurt me. I always thought he was going to. He wasn't like his son. I'm sorry I felt that way about him. Now he's gone.

I'm sorry daddy made me feel that way about Grandpa. It was all daddy's fault. He wanted me to think I was a bad girl. He wanted me to think I was a bad girl. I was not a bad girl! It was not my fault. He was the bad person and now he is dying. I'm glad he is dying. I suppose that does make me a bad girl. He always wanted me to be a bad girl. I told him I hated it. I'm not so little now. I told him it made me sick. I wanted to throw up. He laughed at me and said I liked it. "You like it, don't you! If you didn't like it you wouldn't do it for your dad". I hated it and I hated him. I don't care if it does make me bad—I HATE HIM!!!!

He's a bad man. He will be a bad man when he dies. I get mad at you when you kiss him on the forehead. I want to throw up all over again. But I guess I understand. He is your father. I will not call him my father. So I guess we really aren't one yet, are we? I'm 14 years old. There wasn't only one Little Girl. You never thought of me. Only the Little Girl. Well maybe I hate her too. She got all the attention when we were healing.

You never thought about me. I was the ugly one—not the Little Girl. She was cute. I knew she hurt so I let her get the attention. She needed it more than me. I can always get along. I long to be alone.

I felt guilt over Bonnie. I couldn't have fun when I knew she was unhappy. It was really hard. Daddy paid no attention to her; you know what I mean. I liked Jerry. We did fun things, but I always felt sad for Bonnie. I was never free to be me—me—a person.

I was Bonnie's sister.

I was Penny's protector.

I was Daddy's whore.

I was Mama's cop out.

I was never me.

I wanted to be me. I wanted to be loved for me. I liked Jerry. We had fun. He kissed me. It was different than daddy's kiss. I liked him to kiss me good night. I hated daddy to kiss me. I told him I hated him and I would kill him somehow if he didn't stop. He finally stopped. I don't know why he did. I was happy when he did.

Now I hate him. I cannot forgive him like you did. Please, just let me hate him and be happy when he is dead. Crying doesn't help; the only thing that will help is for him to be dead—dead—dead.

The conversation continued:

Adult Norma:

Norma, am I betraying you when I kiss him on the forehead?

14 Year Old:

Yes, I hate you for that. You don't care about me anymore than anyone else did. You are a fool. You think your mother cares. She knew all along. Don't you remember what she said—he may have done some things—but not all the way.

Yeah, right, she knew. It kept his you know what out of her—that's all she cared about—not me. Poor mama. Bonnie was never strong. Daddy wanting me. I honestly don't know what she thought of me. Penny was and is definitely her favorite. She always was and always will be. She was always her baby. Babies' are not responsible. She's never responsible, she's the baby.

I'm mad at Bonnie—mostly for what she is doing to you. I don't think you should ever talk to her again. But do what you want.

I see the grown up in you and I don't like it. But I don't think I can do anything about it. I never could do anything about anything so I don't know why I should try.

I like Danny. He's good to you. He loves you. I love him for that. You better treat him good because I want him to stay. Don't do anything stupid and lose him.

Do I sound like a brat? Lots of times I feel like one, but don't have the guts to act like one. I really am a coward.

Little Norma—she was never a coward. She fought with him every time—until he mentioned Penny—but then that wasn't being a coward—that was being stupid. She should have let Penny and Bonnie both take care of themselves. They never helped you, have they? What sisters—you sure got stuck with them.

I'm getting tired—I'm still mad. Maybe I will forgive you. Don't be a fool like Little Norma, though.

Be smart—take a vacation instead of going to the bastard's funeral. That would serve them all right.

Bye for now, Norma

Little Norma:

This is Little Norma, it's my turn to talk. Don't mind Norma too much. She's just really mad. It was harder for her than me. I didn't really comprehend all that was happening. I hated it, but I could play with my dolls afterwards. It haunted her. I wanted to kill him for Penny. She wanted to kill him for her. I love her. She will get better. It will just take a little more time. She didn't have anybody or anything. Just love her. She needs it. I don't care if he dies. Whatever! He hasn't bothered me for a long time. Let him go. I don't care.

February 28, 1998

Adult Norma:

Dear Norma Fourteen Year Old. How are you today? I visited with my dad. I didn't kiss him. I was thinking of you. How are you today? I really want to know.

14 Year Old:

Thank you for not kissing him. It makes me feel good that you respect my feelings about that. I don't care how you act about him. It will never change for me, but I know that you have to do what you feel. I'm glad you listen to me and let me tell you how I really feel. I'm not really important for you to understand. I know you don't know how to help me. I never knew how to help me. I guess that's why I always felt so helpless, in a different way than Little Norma. She was always so good. She did everything for everybody. I just couldn't feel that way. I just didn't have that kind of love. I don't know when I lost it. It's just gone. I really don't feel love for anybody. I do feel a lot of anger. I'm mad more for you than for me. I didn't expect any help. Little Norma never got it so why should I, but I did expect more for you. That's why I'm so mad. I'm happy you are spending time with the Perry's. The vacation in Florida will be fun for you. Enjoy yourself, Norma. I didn't. You

deserve it, no, we deserve it. Remember when you have
fun, we have fun. We want to go to the circus.

Adult Norma:

How many of you are there?"

14 Year Old:

Seven. You won't get to all of us maybe. Some are really
too shy to talk to you. They are all Normas.

Adult Norma:

What happened to Penny when she was so sick with the
bleeding? I can't remember. I should. I was, I think, in
high school, living at home. I don't remember. Was that
you then or another Norma?

14 Year Old:

That wasn't me. She can't talk about it. She
remembers, you don't want to. It's not nice. She's
buried pretty deep. We don't see her much. She's really
quiet.

Adult Norma:

Can you tell me how old she is?

14 Year Old:

No. I can't betray anything about her. I love her and
she needs to be left alone. She was hurt very badly and
she doesn't want to talk about it, even to Sherry.
(Sherry is my therapist.)

Adult Norma:

Was Penny aware of the reason for her problem?

14 Year Old:

I don't know.

Adult Norma:

Were there any happy times of your life?

14 Year Old:

Yes, when Jerry and I went out with Jim and Karen. That was fun.

Adult Norma:

Do you want to go now?

14 Year Old:

No, are you tired of me already?

Adult Norma:

No, what do you want to talk about?

14 Year Old:

I don't know. I'm tired of being lonely. I'm always lonely. Jerry's gone and I'm alone. I did it myself. It is not fun being 14, but it's a lot better than being 12. Twelve was awful. I was scared a lot of the time then.

Adult Norma:

Are you the same person as the Twelve Year Old?"

14 Year Old:

Of course, we're all you. Don't you know that?

Adult Norma:

I don't understand all of you. I don't remember much about that time in my life.

14 Year Old:

We remember it all. We have it here for you. Are you sure you want it?

Adult Norma:

I'm not sure I'm ready for it. I need to go now.

14 Year Old:

Okay, it's up to you. Good bye.

CHAPTER 39

GETTING BRAVER

At the end of the last chapter I was too frightened to listen to more.

It took a couple of years, but I think I am ready to move on.

March 22, 2001

Today is Danny's birthday. I figured out why I always have to have his high school picture out. It's just a small one and was getting wrinkled. I backed it on construction paper to make it stronger. I will get a small frame for it.

I believe it is for you, 14-Year-Old Norma. If not, please tell me which one of you like it. A lot has happened since I last talked with you through my journal.

Dad died. I never kissed him again. Even at the funeral. I had too much respect for you.

I have visited Bonnie. Things are better now.

Penny and I spend one day a week with mom.

Penny, mom and I had an outing last week. Stephen, my little grandson was with us. He was in his car seat between mom and Penny. He threw a temper tantrum and hit my mother. He needed to be punished for it. She got mad at him and hit him back. She hit him twice. After the second slap I turned around and looked back at her and saw her hit him right in the center of his face with her open hand. Then she said to him, "You're a brat." I was angry at the slap but when she said, "You're a brat," it made me angrier than the slaps. I said, "He's the baby."

Which one of you said that? I don't think it was the Adult Norma. Please talk to me. I love you all and am ready to meet all of you.

Child:

It was me who answered her. It was so familiar to me. How dare she do that to Stephen! See? She didn't learn anything. I knew she didn't. She wants you to think she is sorry for all your pain, but she could have stopped it if she chose to. It was so much easier for her while he was with all of us. It didn't matter the age. I still hate her. She makes me sick. I get mad when you spend time with her—but—oh well—what the hell.

Adult Norma:

How old are you?

Child:

I'm 14. I try to take care of the little ones. They don't need me as much as they used to. You have helped them a lot. Will you help me too? I want to heal. I want the pain in my head and in my heart to stop. I'm tired of carrying so much of the pain. Please help me.

Adult Norma: "How can I help you?"

14 Year Old:

Talk to Penny, you both need to help me.

Adult Norma:

How can we do that?

14 Year Old:

She will know.

Adult Norma:

I don't know what to do. Give me some more hints.

14 Year Old:

Penny will know how to help me.

Adult Norma: "

Is it about when she was sick?

14 Year Old:

Yes.

Adult Norma:

Was I 14 then?

14 Year Old:

No.

Adult Norma:

Penny is out of town. I really needed to work on memories today. I rented a hotel room to be alone. Can we do something else?

14 Year Old:

Okay.

Adult Norma:

Okay, what do you want to talk about?

14 Year Old:

Merrill Nye. I loved him and Gladys. They loved me for me. That was another happy time for me. He let me drive his car. It was a younger me. I'm all of them rolled into one. They are separate, but I feel them all. They know me, but I feel them.

Adult Norma:

Are you the oldest or are there older Norma's?

14 Year Old:

There is an older one—but she is deep—very deep. She hurts a lot. She wants help now. I know she will talk to you soon. She has to know she is safe. She's very frightened and shy. She knew Dick. He wanted her to be someone she wasn't. He wanted to marry her, make her into a preacher's wife. At first she thought she could. It would get her away from here. She liked him, but when he went away to the army she knew, once again, she couldn't be what someone else made her. Not the real her. She had to be her!

Adult Norma:

Tell her I want to talk to her. I will believe all she tells me and will love her and be kind to her. Is she the one who makes it hard for me to enjoy making love with Dan?

14 Year Old:

Don't pin that on her. She has enough problems!

Adult Norma:

Did she like her tan suit and brown shoes? I remember I did?

14 Year Old:

Yes, it made her feel grown up and pretty and strong enough to kill the bastard. He knew it to. He was truly afraid of her. She threatened him one day and he believed her. He never touched her again. It was so good to be free! Never to worry about him again!

Adult Norma:

Then why is she so afraid to talk and have you do the talking for her?

14 Year Old:

I will try to get her to talk. Take a break.

16 Year Old:

I am 16 years old. I feel more sophisticated than the others. I like Dick. I'm sorry we aren't together. He's a good man. His parents are nice. I was always afraid of his father, but not now. His mom is sweet and caring and sick. I think that's why I know I can't marry Dick. I don't want to be like his mom, and I'm afraid an older Dick would be like his father. His sisters are sweet and I would enjoy them being my sisters. They would love me and expect nothing from me. I'm sad he's gone. I know it is right.

Adult Norma:

You sound like you have your head together. Do you have any problems?

16 Year Old:

Do I have problems? Are you crazy? We all have problems. That bastard made our lives a hell and you asked me a stupid question like that? Boy, where do you get off, so holier than me?

I'm sorry. There seems to be two of me. How do you like that? Not only all of these Normas, but two of one of them?

I have so much anger. I really wanted to kill him. If I did I could say it was to protect the others and I mean the other Normas. I don't mess with Penny and Bonnie any more. I don't care.

(The 16 Year Old went into details about the hatred of her father here, but I, the Adult Norma, decided to edit it out.)

You have great kids. They never had to face what I did. You protected them. Thank you. I love them all.

Good day for now, Big Norma

March 23, 2001—1:00 A.M

I am still at the hotel. All alone tonight. I've eaten too much—not exercised—but tomorrow I will go back to my routine.

Adult Norma:

Are any of you ready to talk to me again? I'm never sure if you want to talk. I'm always surprised at how it happens. If I were an author, I would think I was imagining it all. But I am not an author and I'm not imagining it. I want you to know when you talk to me you can control my hand. It seems to come more from there than from my mind. I love hearing from you. I have to admit, Big Norma, some of your language was difficult for me to write. I'm much more spiritual now than I was a while ago. I'm not asking you to change. Stay who you are, and please continue to share with me all you want me to know.

Little Norma, I found a doll like the one you used to hold. She is on my bed every day. I'm sure you know that. I found some clothes today that I think will fit her. I might buy them tomorrow. Let me know if you really want them.

I'm a little afraid of all of you. I know I need to know you better and I want to know you better. But it is not always easy. I'm being very honest with you tonight. Maybe you need to hear from me tonight. I can be a little afraid and still love you. I'm sure you are afraid of things also.

I'm very curious about 12-year-old Norma. I know nothing about her. Twelve Year Old, are you in the 7th grade? I believe that is when we moved back from Texas. That year is so faint in my memory. Of all the years I, remember that the least. I don't even remember that teacher's name. Was it Mr. Potter? Who were my friends? I think they were Judy and Nancy and Carol. But I don't think I was close to any of them.

When you are ready to talk I want to listen. Maybe tomorrow if you will. I'm too tired tonight. Good night to all of you. I might be awake most of the night. I'm often awake all night.

I love you all. I'm going to try to figure out seven of you.

1. 3 Year Old   Little Little Norma

2. 4 Year Old   Little Norma

3. 6 Year Old

4. 8 Year Old

5. 12 Year Old

6. 14 Year Old

7. 16 Year Old   Big Norma

March 23, 2001— Noon

Adult Norma:

Dear Normas, I checked out of my room. First I exercised, soaked in the hot tub and then got ready to leave. I drove to Lexington and back. I need to be home in a couple of hours to babysit Stephen. That gives me about one hour if anyone wants to talk.

I think the ones I know least about are 8 Year Old and 12 Year Old. Are there those ages?

The weather is beautiful today. The ice is gone. It is so peaceful now. It seems I have the whole lake to myself.

I have been thinking what I want now for my life. I want to be happy; I want my house paid for; and I want to take a vacation. Enough of me. I'm inviting anyone who wants to, to talk to me. I love you all.

12 Year Old:

Okay, here I am. I am your 12 Year Old. I am not happy. I am scared. I hate the old man. He makes me sick. I was so happy when he died. I don't have to look at him again. The older he got, the uglier he looked. Yes, I can see what is going on now. I see it through my 12-year-old eyes, but I see it. I can talk with you as an adult, though. So don't confuse me with the older ones.

I really love Penny. I am so scared for her. She has been sick. Daddy took her to a doctor. I don't think mama knew about it. I don't want to talk too much about it. Bonnie was good to Penny. I think she understood more than I do. I love Penny. I love Bonnie.

Adult Norma:

I'm getting confused. I keep thinking Sparlingville, but at 12, weren't we living in Texas?

12 Year Old:

Yes, for awhile. Then we came back here. Grandpa was sick. Mama didn't want to stay in Texas. I liked it there. I liked our church and our school. I liked our house. I liked the weather. We didn't see much of Merrill and Gladys though and I was sorry for that.

Adult Norma:

Can you tell me anything about the 7th grade?

12 Year Old:

I hated that year. Grandpa died. I loved Grandpa so much. I didn't want him to die. I cried and cried. Mama held me while I cried for Grandpa. She was nice then. I liked her holding me.

Adult Norma:

What was school like? What were my classes?

12 Year Old:

That year I took homemaking. Mrs. Sommers is our teacher. We cook for part of the year and sew for another part. I like the cooking, the sewing is hard for me. Judy helps me a lot. Then we have gym class. I play ping pong instead of dressing out for it. I just hate doing it, and the teacher never said anything. Only I did get a D at the end of the marking period. I don't care, though. This is my first year that we move from classroom to classroom. The bell rings and we change classes.

Adult Norma:

Why are you so scared this year?

12 Year Old:

We moved home from Texas. We are back in the same house. Daddy works in the barn and smells all oily. I hate that smell. He still comes to me. I feel too big for doing that. It doesn't seem right to me. I know it is bad, but he says I like to do it and it makes him happy so what's the harm. He talks to me more now. It gives me a good feeling, but I know it is bad. I don't understand these feelings inside of me. Why do I feel this way? Daddy says I'm supposed to feel good. Then why do I feel ugly to?

I don't hate daddy, I know I'm supposed to but what he does feels good and I know that makes me really bad. I don't know what to do. I want to talk to mama, but I know she will be really mad, and she is sad about her daddy dying now.

I don't understand the feelings inside of me. I think I want to die. I can't keep feeling this way. I really want to die. I don't know how to do it. I know I'm not supposed to hurt myself. My angels told me that a long time ago. I feel so dirty inside of me. Nothing can make me clean. I wish I could swallow bleach and clean my insides out.

I must do something to me so that when daddy does that to me it doesn't make me feel good. I hate him for it, but I want it. There I said it. Do you hate me now? I wanted him to do it to me. That is why I hate him so much. I am such a terrible person. I don't deserve to live. I should hide forever for these feelings I get. I don't know what to do. I have to do something so it doesn't feel good. Maybe God will make it awful for me.

14 Year Old:

That's enough for now. Leave her (the 12 year old) alone. She can't take much more. I'm 14. I protect her. I wasn't there when she had those feelings. Hate will take it away. She didn't hate him enough. I do. She always feels guilty. The guilt never goes away for her. Like her mama said, it was bad and dirty and awful. She doesn't understand what her mama says and what her daddy does.

I just hate them both. It is much easier.

He still does it to me but I don't even feel it anymore. I feel nothing.

I showed him and his bitch. I hate them both so much. But I feel in control so I can stand it. I'm me! They can't take that away from me.

He can **** me, and she can hit me, but I don't feel it any more.

I feel nothing. That is so good and so free. NOTHING! NOTHING! NOTHING!

CHAPTER 40

ADULT NORMA

2009

I am the adult Norma all the time now. Occasionally I feel my Little Girls, but it is a good feeling of being young again for a little while.

I remember the day my 16 Year Old left for good. We both knew she was leaving. I was sitting beside the St. Clair River. She and I were talking through my journal. I was sad because I knew she was going. She said goodbye and was gone. I felt her leave. I don't know why she had to leave me.

I think that Norma 14 Year Old is still part of me. I believe that her anger and sadness are gone.

I know I still have some of the Little Ones inside of me because I still enjoy coloring at times and I still dress my dolls once in a while. My 7-year-old granddaughter, Kylee, and I like to take walks while she pushes the doll carriage. I enjoy it as much as she does as it gives me the feeling of doing it.

In April of 2002 my mom became very ill. She came to live with me. We brought her bedroom furniture to my home so she would feel like she was at home. She was only there for two weeks before she died. Many people loved her and she had the opportunity to say goodbye to them.

About four years after she died, Penny said to me, "You took it really good when mom admitted she did know all along." I didn't know what she was talking about. She went on to say that, on her deathbed, mom admitted to knowing about the abuse. Penny and I were with her and she quietly said, "I did know," but I didn't hear it. I'm glad I didn't. I don't know if I could have dealt with it then. Now, it is just another proof that I was not crazy all those days of my healing.

They are both gone now. I feel no hatred or animosity toward them. I love them.

I have a good relationship with both of my sisters now. I think they both believe what went on. We don't talk about it.

I am so glad that the Little Girls have healed enough for me to feel good about them and about my parents and sisters.

I am really very lucky. I have a wonderful life. I have a wonderful, loving husband, five grown children, two sons-in-law, two daughters-in-law, and 11 fantastic grandchildren.

EPILOGUE

February 13, 2013

This is the last of my adding to my journal. I am finally bringing it to a close. I remember one day in my healing, I mentioned a few things I wanted. I now have some of them. I have my home paid for and almost restored to look like it did in 1880. I have my lovely camper that I love to use for vacations and to spend time alone when I feel the need. My children do not all live next door to me like I wanted, but they are all within driving distance for me to visit whenever I like. I am still married to the most wonderful man in the world. How I love him! He is truly the hardest working, most forgiving, most nonjudgmental man I have ever met and he loves me! How lucky I am!

My baby sister, Penny, passed away this year. I was very blessed to be able to spend many hours by her side during her last days. My older sister, Bonnie, is editing this book for me. We are very close again.

Throughout my healing journey, I kept trying to find me. My journal helped me to discover that I have always been me, and even more important, that now:

I **UNDERSTAND** me.

CPSIA information can be obtained
at www.ICGtesting.com
Printed in the USA
FFOW02n0344200716
26028FF

9 780615 775173